EVERYDAY WISDOM FOR EVERLASTING LIFE

A Study of Proverbs

Jack W. Hayford
with
R. Samuel Thorpe

THOMAS NELSON PUBLISHERS
Nashville • Atlanta • London • Vancouver

Proverbs:
Everyday Wisdom for Everlasting Life

Published in Nashville, Tennessee, by Thomas Nelson, Inc.

Printed in the United States of America
5 6 7 8 — 01 00 99

CONTENTS

Everyday Wisdom for Everlasting Life: A Study of Proverbs is one of a series of study guides that focus exciting, discovery-geared coverage of Bible book and power themes—all prompting toward dynamic, Holy Spirit-filled living.

About the Executive Editor

JACK W. HAYFORD, noted pastor, teacher, writer, and composer, is the Executive Editor of the complete series, working with the publisher in the conceiving and developing of each of the books.

Dr. Hayford is Senior Pastor of The Church On The Way, the First Foursquare Church of Van Nuys, California. He and his wife, Anna, have four married children, all of whom are active in either pastoral ministry or vital church life. As General Editor of the *Spirit-Filled Life® Bible,* Pastor Hayford led a four-year project, which has resulted in the availability of one of today's most practical and popular study Bibles. He is author of more than twenty books, including *A Passion for Fullness, The Beauty of Spiritual Language, Rebuilding the Real You*, and *Prayer Is Invading the Impossible*. His musical compositions number over four hundred songs, including the widely sung "Majesty."

About the Writer

R. SAMUEL THORPE is a college professor at Oral Roberts Unversity in Tulsa, Oklahoma. He teaches Bible and Theology courses as well as serving as mentor to Christian Education and Pastoral Ministry students. Samuel has written several books and articles, primarily for courses taken by ORU students, such as *Good Writers, A Handbook for Basic Biblical Exegesis,* and *Poetic Literature of the Old Testament.*

Dr. Thorpe received his Ph.D. from the University of Tulsa in educational administration and research, and his Master's degree in Bible from Oral Roberts University. He and his wife, Chrissy, who are together writing a book on family and children, have raised four children: James and John, students at ORU; Ben, an artist soon to study at Savannah College of Art and Design; and Anna, a high school student.

Of this contributor, the Executive Editor has remarked: "Dr. Thorpe is yet another example of the fine scholars the Holy Spirit is raising up in the academic comunity, who keep a warm heart for God and help ignite the same in others."

THE GIFT THAT KEEPS ON GIVING

Who doesn't like presents? Whether they come wrapped in colorful paper and beautiful bows, or brown paper bags closed and tied at the top with old shoestring. Kids and adults of all ages love getting and opening presents.

But even this moment of surprise and pleasure can be marked by dread and fear. All it takes is for these words to appear: "Assembly Required. Instructions Enclosed." How we hate these words! They taunt us, tease us, beckon us to try to challenge them, all the while knowing that they have the upper hand. If we don't understand the instructions, or if we ignore them and try to put the gift together ourselves, more than likely, we'll only assemble frustration and anger. What we felt about our great gift—all the joy, anticipation, and wonder—will vanish. And they will never return, at least not to that pristine state they had before we realized that *we* had to assemble our present with instructions *no consumer* will ever understand.

One of the most precious gifts God has given us is His Word, the Bible. Wrapped in the glory and sacrifice of His Son and delivered by the power and ministry of His Spirit, it is a treasured gift—one the family of God has preserved and protected for centuries as a family heirloom. It promises that it is the gift that keeps on giving, because the Giver it reveals is inexhaustible in His love and grace.

Tragically, though, fewer and fewer people, even those who number themselves among God's everlasting family, are opening this gift and seeking to understand what it's all about and how to use it. They often feel intimidated by it. It requires some assembly, and its instructions are hard to comprehend sometimes. How does the Bible fit together anyway? What does Genesis have to do with Revelation? Who are Abraham and Moses, and what is their relationship to Jesus and Paul? And what about the works of the Law and the works of faith? What are they all about, and how do they fit together, if at all?

And what does this ancient book have to say to us who are looking toward the twenty-first century? Will taking the time and energy to understand its instructions and to fit it all together really help you and me? Will it help us better understand who we are, what the future holds, how we can better live here and now? Will it really help us in our personal relationships, in our marriages and families, in our jobs? Can it give us more than just advice on how to handle crises? the death of a loved one? the financial fallout of losing a job? catastrophic illness? betrayal by a friend? the seduction of our values? the abuses of the heart and soul? Will it allay our fears and calm our restlessness and heal our wounds? Can it really get us in touch with the same power that gave birth to the universe? that parted the Red Sea? that raised Jesus from the stranglehold of the grave? Can we really find unconditional love, total forgiveness, and genuine healing in its pages?

Yes. Yes. Without a shred of doubt.

The *Spirit-Filled Life® Bible Discovery Guide* series is designed to help you unwrap, assemble, and enjoy all God has for you in the pages of Scripture. It will focus your time and energy on the books of the Bible, the people and places they describe, and the themes and life applications that flow thick from its pages like honey oozing from a beehive.

So you can get the most out of God's Word, this series has a number of helpful features. Each study guide has no more than fourteen lessons, each arranged so you can plumb the depths or skim the surface, depending on your needs and interests.

The study guides also contain six major lesson features, each marked by a symbol and heading for easy identification.

WORD WEALTH

The WORD WEALTH feature provides important definitions of key terms.

BEHIND THE SCENES

BEHIND THE SCENES supplies information about cultural beliefs and practices, doctrinal disputes, business trades, and the like that illuminate Bible passages and teachings.

AT A GLANCE

The AT A GLANCE feature uses maps and charts to identify places and simplify themes or positions.

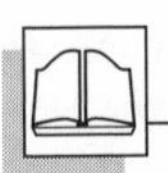

BIBLE EXTRA

Because this study guide focuses on a book of the Bible, you will find a BIBLE EXTRA feature that guides you into Bible dictionaries, Bible encyclopedias, and other resources that will enable you to glean more from the Bible's wealth if you want something extra.

PROBING THE DEPTHS

Another feature, PROBING THE DEPTHS, will explain controversial issues raised by particular lessons and cite Bible passages and other sources to which you can turn to help you come to your own conclusions.

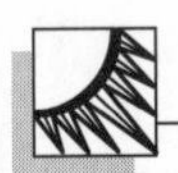

FAITH ALIVE

Finally, each lesson contains a FAITH ALIVE feature. Here the focus is, So what? Given what the Bible says, what does it mean for my life? How can it impact my day-to-day needs, hurts, relationships, concerns, and whatever else is important to me? FAITH ALIVE will help you see and apply the practical relevance of God's literary gift.

As you'll see, these guides supply space for you to answer the study and life-application questions and exercises. You may, however, want to record all your answers, or just the overflow from your study or application, in a separate notebook or journal. This would be especially helpful if you think you'll dig into the BIBLE EXTRA features. Because the exercises in this feature are optional and they can be expanded as far as you want to take them, we have not allowed writing space for them in this study guide. So you may want to have a notebook or journal handy for recording your discoveries while working through to this feature's riches.

The Bible study method used in this series revolves around four basic steps: observation, interpretation, correlation, and application. Observation answers the question, What does the text say? Interpretation deals with, What does the text mean?—not with what it means to you or me, but what it meant to its original readers. Correlation asks, What light do other Scripture passages shed on this text? And application, the goal of Bible study, poses the question, How should my life change in response to the Holy Spirit's teaching of this text?

If you have used a Bible much before, you know that it comes in a variety of translations and paraphrases. Although you can use any of them with profit as you work through the *Spirit-Filled Life® Bible Discovery Guide* series, when Bible passages or words are cited, you will find they are from the New King James Version of the Bible. Using this translation with this series will make your study easier, but it's certainly not necessary.

The only resources you need to complete and apply these study guides are a heart and mind open to the Holy Spirit, a prayerful attitude, and a pencil and a Bible. Of course, you may draw upon other sources, such as commentaries, dictionaries, encyclopedias, atlases, and concordances, and you'll even find some optional exercises that will guide you into these sources. But these are extras, not necessities. These study guides are comprehensive enough to give you all you need to gain a good, basic understanding of the Bible book being covered and how you can apply its themes and counsel to your life.

A word of warning, though. By itself, Bible study will not transform your life. It will not give you power, peace, joy, comfort, hope, and a number of other gifts God longs for you to unwrap and enjoy. Through Bible study, you will grow in your understanding of the Lord, His kingdom and your place in it, and those things are essential. But you need more. You need to rely on the Holy Spirit to guide your study and your application of the Bible's truths. He, Jesus promised, was sent to teach us "all things" (John 14:26; cf. 1 Cor. 2:13). So as you use this series to guide you through Scripture, bathe your study time in prayer, asking the Spirit of God to illuminate the text, enlighten your mind, humble your will, and comfort your heart. He will never let you down.

My prayer and goal for you is that as you unwrap and begin to explore God's Book for living His way, the Holy Spirit will fill every fiber of your being to the joy and power God longs to give all His children. So read on. Be diligent. Stay open and submissive to Him. You will not be disappointed. He promises you!

Lesson 1/Let's Begin
(1:1–7)

"You know, Mother used to say. . . ." We all know sayings and bits of wisdom passed down to us by parents and friends. Remember

A penny saved is a penny earned.
A bird in the hand is worth two in the bush.
God helps those who help themselves.
Look before you leap.
People who live in glass houses shouldn't throw stones.

What are some other wise sayings you recall from your childhood?

These little sayings are proverbs, little packages of guidance for life, which are surprisingly effective and helpful. They still shape our behavior. We see signs in the gym or health club that say "No pain, no gain," or "It's not over 'til it's over." Some of our successful businesses use sayings such as "Don't change horses in midstream," or "If at first you don't succeed, try, try again," to promote their products. We build our relationships on such ideas as "Variety is the spice of life," and "Blood is thicker than water." Why are we so affected by these little ditties? Probably because these bits of wisdom are practical and useful in certain situations and they are easy to remember.

We Need Help

The ancient Hebrew people, like most cultures, also had proverbs to live by. They used these sayings to teach their young people what to expect from life and how to deal with it, just as our proverbs do for us. Read these next passages from the Book of Proverbs and note the purposes for proverbs, as well as the benefits received by learning them.

Proverbs 1:1–9

Proverbs 2:1–9

Proverbs 3:1–4, 21–26

Proverbs 4:1–10

The Book of Proverbs groups several collections of wise sayings which God inspired and directed to be kept in written form. From these proverbs we can learn how to deal with life, even before some situations occur. The way of wisdom is to learn and live, not live and learn. God has provided all the help we need to live a righteous, abundant life—His Spirit, His Word, and His people (see 2 Pet. 1:3, 4). As part of His written Word, Proverbs aims at wisdom for daily living. The ultimate result of following God's ways is the experience, even now, of everlasting life.

Jesus loved proverbs and used many such sayings to teach His disciples. When His hometown friends refused to believe in Him, He responded with a proverb: "A prophet is not without honor except in his own country and in his own house" (Matt. 13:57). He explained to His disciples that people misunderstood John the Baptist's ministry as well as His own, again with a proverb: "Wisdom is justified by her children"

(Matt. 11:19). On yet another occasion, when He taught about His second coming, Jesus used a proverb which was probably as well-known to the people then as "Where there's smoke, there's fire" is to us today. Jesus used this earthy proverb to underscore the sad fall of Jerusalem near the time of the final judgment: "For wherever the carcass is, there the eagles will be gathered together" (Matt. 24:28).

Word Wealth

The word *proverb* comes to English from a Latin word that means "a word, speech, or discourse." The Hebrew word is *mashal*, which includes the core idea of "comparison." Indeed, we shall see that most proverbs compare a positive action with a negative one, such as

"The hand of the diligent shall rule,
But the slothful man shall be a slave" (Prov. 12:24).

Understood broadly, the biblical proverb also includes riddles and word puzzles. Biblical and Eastern literature frequently use the proverb as a literary technique to make their writings enjoyable and memorable. People of all nations have found satisfaction and pleasure learning to solve riddles and other word problems.

God Is a Great Guide

Proverbs illustrate certain truths that should be applied in specific situations of life. This principle is important for us as we interpret the proverbs, because the social situation, or *context*, determines what the particular proverb means. Consider some modern proverbs, such as

He who hesitates is lost.
Look before you leap.

Silence is golden.
The squeaky wheel gets the grease.[1]

Notice in these pairs of sayings that the principles seem to contradict themselves. First, hesitation is bad, but caution is good. Then silence is praised, but noise gets attention to your needs.

The reason these modern proverbs sound contradictory is that we have arbitrarily grouped them. If we take each one separately, in its own situation, we can agree to its wisdom.

The biblical Proverbs portray truth about life, but we misunderstand them if we neglect the context of each one. For example, in Proverbs 25:2, "it is the glory of God to conceal a thing . . . ," yet the New Testament indicates that God's glory is revealed in the universe and in Christ (Rom. 1:18–20; Heb. 1:1–3). Is there a conflict? Not when we consider the rest of the passage, "but the glory of kings is to search out a matter." Now we can realize the meaning of the saying.

Earthly rulers have the responsibility to make their actions and laws clear and understandable to all the people in their kingdoms. They also must seek the truth so that justice is done and order is kept in the realm (Rom. 13:1–7; 1 Tim. 2:2; 1 Pet. 2:13–14). On the one hand, God is glorified by being merciful to sinners and, through Christ, covering their sins—removing them and remembering them no more. Yet on the other hand, much about God is mysterious and wonderful. He is glorified when we recognize His majesty, that He is high above us and greater than anything we can comprehend. With these explanations, we better understand these verses and see that there is no conflict between Proverbs and the New Testament concerning what God conceals or reveals. We simply have to consider the contexts of the passages.

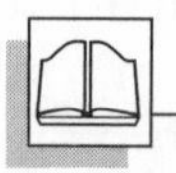

BIBLE EXTRA

Read the following pairs of passages, and summarize the teaching of each individual proverb. Then think about what the New Testament teaches on the subject and write what the New Testament verses mean to you.

Proverbs 26:4 and
Proverbs 26:5
(See Philip. 3:17–19; James 3:1–12)

Proverbs 24:13 and
Proverbs 25:16
(See 1 Cor. 8 and 10:14–33)

Proverbs 27:13 and
Proverbs 11:15
(See 2 Cor. 6:14–18; Gal. 6:1–10)

Proverbs 18:11 and
Proverbs 11:28
(See James 2:1–13; Acts 8:3; 16:19)

AT A GLANCE

King Solomon (970 B.C.) is well-known for his wisdom, a gift given to him from God (I Kings 3:5–14). Most of the Proverbs are his, though there are a few other people who contributed some. The Proverbs were collected during the reigns of the Judean kings from Solomon through Hezekiah (720 B.C.).[2]

WHEN THE PROVERBS WERE WRITTEN AND COMPILED

Moses 1500 B.C.	Reign of Solomon 970–931 B.C.	Hezekiah 720 B.C.	Ezra 500 B.C.

1500 1300 1100 900 700 500

BIBLE EXTRA

Proverbs is part of the division of the Bible known as Wisdom Literature, which includes Psalms, Job, Song of

Solomon, and Ecclesiastes. These books provide us with a better understanding of some of the most practical and down-to-earth truths about life. Much of wisdom literature is written in poetry, which communicates emotion, so that we can experience the feelings of the characters of the Old Testament and the heart of God.

The Psalms express all the deep emotions humans possess, from great sadness to triumphant joy. The deep suffering of Job, the pity and helplessness of his friends, and the majestic compassion of God jump out at us from the pages of the book of Job. Song of Solomon celebrates the love of husband and wife, and Ecclesiastes reveals the vanity and frustration of a life without faith in God.

Wisdom literature focuses on daily human experience in the good world God made for us. Wisdom is an attribute of God, part of His divinity, given by Him to us so that we might live abundant, satisfying lives (Prov. 2:6). When you read wisdom in the Bible, you don't usually find stories about God's judgment on sinful humanity in the last days, the coming of the Messiah, or God's actions in history to save His people. Instead, you find guidance for everyday life.

Teach Us!

We need to be taught so that we can distinguish good advice and truth from poor counsel and falsehood (Prov. 1:2). Parents today are striving to raise children who are fully equipped to deal with a world full of many different ideas about what is right and wrong. Opportunities to make money are everywhere, but are they all legal, ethical, and God-honoring? Even different Christians disagree about how to deal with certain social and political issues. How are we supposed to know how to respond? The Bible is God's revealed truth, and Proverbs in particular will help us with the practical side of life.

The Proverbs show us how to deal respectfully and intelligently with each other in social, business, and political affairs (Prov. 1:1–3).

Read the following passages and list the ways the Word of God helps us recognize truth and falsehood.

Proverbs 1:10–19 (ways of sinners)

Proverbs 2:1–15 (ways of wisdom)

Proverbs 3:5–12 (ways of God)

We learn in order to obtain wisdom, the intelligent use of knowledge. Proverbs seeks to impart such wisdom to people of all ages. Proverbs gives youth a standard by which all decisions can be weighed, to spare them troubles and heartaches, as well as to propel them toward successful lives (1:4). Proverbs adds to the wisdom of the mature so they may live well, as well as guide others to follow God's ways. Life poses many curious, hard-to-understand problems. Proverbs will enlighten us and give us discernment about these puzzles. God does not want us to live in the dark, to be victims of vanity and foolishness.

Proverbs is a book that provides the people of God with practical wisdom in easy-to-remember capsules of truth that show us

- what situations exist in the world,
- the wise responses we should make to these situations, and
- the benefits of living by the principles that please God.

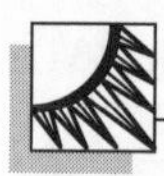

FAITH ALIVE

Proverbs has much to offer you! Before going further in this study, list in Column A below three specific situations in your life where you want the wisdom God would provide you through prayerful study of Proverbs.

A. The Situation and the Answer or Guidance I'm Seeking	B. Proverbs That May Apply and What Each Teaches	C. Summary: What I Believe God May Be Guiding Me to Do
1.		
2.		
3.		

Insert a bookmark at this page. Then, *as you continue your study*, list in Column B the reference of all Proverbs you study that seem to apply to the situations listed in Column A. With the references, write a brief summary of the teaching of each proverb listed. Throughout your study, *pray* regularly for God to supply the wisdom you need (see James 1:5–8). As you study and pray, when you begin to see a personal application of each proverb, write these applications in Column C.

God Is First!

How do we begin to become wise? The beginning of Proverbs tells us: We come to God; we respect and reverence Him in all submission and humility: "The fear of the Lord is the beginning of knowledge, but fools despise wisdom and instruction" (Prov. 1:7). To "fear" the Lord means to acknowledge His great power, His complete authority over us and all creation, and His terrible hatred of sin. But it also means for us to acknowledge His tremendous love and mercy toward us, and His goodness (Ps. 145:3–20). Life has no meaning without God. He is the point, the reason, for all existence. We come first to Him for help, for guidance, for training (2 Tim. 3:16–17), so that we may live abundant lives (John 10:10), serving God in good works (John 14:11–14; 15:1–10), and leading others to His grace and salvation (Acts 1:8).

What are some ways we show God reverence and fear?

Proverbs 3:5–8

Proverbs 3:9, 10

Proverbs 3:11, 12

Proverbs 5:21–23

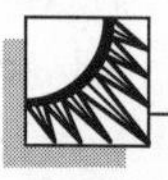

FAITH ALIVE

Proverbs reaches beyond our human games to show us the truth about ourselves and what are the best ways to live. God is the focus of Proverbs and He should be the focus of our lives as well. He is our Creator; He inspired the book and is the Person best able to show us the right paths. Look up the references below, and, following the examples, summarize what each reference presents as either the world's or God's way.

World's Way (Prov. 1:11, 12) Power over other people

God's Way (Prov. 3:3–8) Humility, selflessness

World's Way (Prov. 8:36) ______________________

God's Way (Prov. 8:32–35) ______________________

World's Way (Prov. 10:18) ______________________

God's Way (Prov. 10:20, 21, 31, 32) ______________

World's Way (Prov. 21:25, 26) ___________________

God's Way (Prov. 6:6–8) _______________________

1. Rod Evans and Irwin Berent, from an article in *Reader's Digest* (October, 1993), condensed from their book *Getting Your Word's Worth*, (New York: Warner Books, 1993).

2. Jack Hayford (Gen. Ed.), *Hayford's Bible Handbook*, (Nashville: Thomas Nelson, 1995), 154.

Lesson 2/Wisdom Is Wonderful
(1:8—9:18)

"Oh, look Angie!" Heather pointed excitedly to the shelf in the store where the latest CD of her favorite musical group was displayed.

"Yeah," Angie retorted, "that's the new one. I got it yesterday, and it's awesome."

With trembling hands and heavy heartbeats, Heather tenderly picked the CD from the shelf. She stared lovingly at the cover, then surveyed the back for the names of all the songs.

"Oh, no! It's got 'How Can You Be That Way' on it!" Heather nearly screamed with delight.

"Uh, huh . . . and 'Meet Me Tomorrow' too," replied Angie, as she began to softly hum the tune.

"Well, I've gotta get this CD," said Heather in a dramatic tone. "I'd feel so left out without it."

"Okay," said Angie, "I'm going over to cosmetics. Meet you there."

Heather opened her purse, but when she counted all her cash, the total was short of the cost of the CD. But she just had to have it! Today! I can't wait for two more weeks, she thought. The store might sell out of them by then. She couldn't borrow from Angie; she already owed her friend $10 anyway.

Heather carefully looked all around the store and, when she was sure no one was watching, she slipped the CD into her purse. Heather immediately felt fear and guilt, but she wanted, no, she *needed*, that CD so much.

When she and Angie finished shopping and reached the front entrance of the store, two stern-looking men stopped them.

"Young lady," growled the taller man, "let's have a look

"Young lady," growled the taller man, "let's have a look in your purse, please."

Heather actually benefited greatly by being caught for her crime. Otherwise, she might have developed an entire lifestyle of deception, stealing, and lying. She lived and learned. But if she were wiser, she would have *learned and lived*, avoiding the high cost of tuition in the school of unwise experience. If Heather had only studied Proverbs and taken it to heart, she would have known to flee even the suggestion of such behavior. She would have known that the smart way to live is by God's wisdom and saved herself much trouble.

Trouncing Temptation (1:8–19; 6:1–19)

Read the following passages and complete each item. As you continue your study of Proverbs, note the advice it offers you for overcoming the temptations it discusses.

Proverbs 1:8–9. What do these verses imply that we may be tempted not to hear or keep?

Proverbs 1:10–19. Peer pressure may tempt us to ______ (v. 11) and to _______ (v. 13). The basic temptation is that of being _______ (v. 19a). Those who give in to that temptation face what ironic result? (v. 19b, also v. 18)

According to v. 15, what is the wise response to such enticement?

Proverbs 6:1–5 portrays action that, at first glance, seems completely charitable. What is this action, and in what way is it unwise?

According to 6:3–5, what should a person do to escape such a snare? What wrong attitude would keep a person from doing what is needed to secure release?

Proverbs 6:6–11 describes what temptation?

What is noteworthy about the actions of the ant?

According to 6:10–11, what is the preventable result of giving in to this temptation?

What does this passage assume about who is primarily responsible for a person's basic material welfare?

Proverbs 6:12–19 lists seven attitudes and actions God hates. List each one, then for each, answer these questions: How does this attitude or action undermine the well-being of a community? Where else in Proverbs 1:8–19 and 6:1–15 is this attitude or action referred to? How does that reference help clarify why God hates this attitude or action?

1.

2.

3.

4.

5.

6.

7.

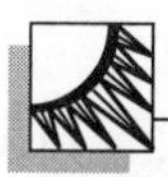

FAITH ALIVE

From all these temptations, which pull at you most strongly?

What advice does Proverbs offer for each of these?

What can you do to follow that advice better from now on?

BIBLE EXTRA

Summarize what each Scripture teaches about how to deal with temptation.

1 Corinthians 10:13

Romans 6:1–7

Romans 8:12–14

1 John 1:6—2:6

The Smart Choice (1:20–33; 8:1—9:18)

In Proverbs 1:20–33 and 8:1—9:18, Solomon uses a literary technique called personification, which means giving an idea a personality and having it behave in human ways. This technique gives us a better picture of an abstract idea, in this case, of wisdom. Wisdom, a gift from God available through the Scriptures, from mature fellow Christians, and from the Spirit of Wisdom, is "out there," in the world, ready to be received by the humble, seeking person. In fact, Proverbs portrays Wisdom as actively seeking to guide people in the ways of life. Yet, as Proverbs 1:20–33 describes, many refuse to receive, listen to, or obey Wisdom's call. But those who do receive numerous benefits, as Proverbs 2 and 3 and much of the rest of Proverbs shows.

Read Proverbs 1:20–33 and 8:1—9:18.

List the ways Wisdom has tried to get people's attention.

List the ways people have refused Wisdom.

List the consequences for refusing Wisdom.

According to Proverbs 2:31, instead of receiving God's active, direct judgment, what do those receive who reject Wisdom in favor of foolishness?

BIBLE EXTRA

Proverbs is concerned with practical matters, with "street smarts," we might say. It emphasizes the general, usual consequences for wise or foolish behavior. While God is always the beginning point for all advice Proverbs gives, Proverbs does not stress God's spectacular interventions in life (such as the Exodus or the deliverance of the three Hebrew children from Nebuchadnezzar's fire) nearly as much as it stresses the more or less natural consequences for cooperating with or rejection God's guidance for living well.

This stress on natural consequences is expressed clearly in Proverbs 1:31. Compare this view with the well-known passage in Romans that describes God's wrath (Rom. 1:18–32). How are the Proverbs—natural consequences and the Romans—God's wrath views similar? How do they differ?

What does this comparison suggest to you about how God is free to work through what we call "the natural order" both to bless and to judge, apart from what we think of as His supernatural, miraculous works?

WORD WEALTH

The Book of Proverbs is about practical wisdom, which has many dimensions. The Hebrew word *chokmah* in Proverbs 1:2 means to be skillful,[1] to have dexterity, to be skilled in art.[2] But in Proverbs 1:3 the Hebrew word is *sakal*. This word means to be circumspect, intelligent, prudent, successful,[3] to have knowledge (Job 39:17), to be inventive and creative (Ex. 31:2, 5). The word can also have specifically religious meanings, such as to know the will of God and seek to do what is right (Ps. 90:12), or ungodly meanings, such as to shrewdly manipulate people or subtly maneuver situations for bad reasons (Ex. 1:10; 1 Cor. 2:6).[4]

What does Proverbs 2:7 teach us about wisdom?

These words make us realize that wisdom involves not only knowledge but the proper use of that knowledge in skillful, perceptive, and prudent ways. Solomon allows us a choice, the smart one or the stupid one; get wisdom for a happy successful life, or be foolish and reap trouble (8:33–36).

BIBLE EXTRA

Read the following passages and respond to each item.

1. Who or what in the New Testament possesses wisdom to a noteworthy degree?(Matt. 13:54; Luke 2:40, 52; 1 Cor. 1:23–24)

2. "Wisdom" is used in some passages to refer to something quite different from what it means in Proverbs. Describe worldly wisdom based on these Scriptures.

1 Corinthians 1:17–31

James 3:13–16

3. According to the following Scriptures, what is godly wisdom like, and how do you get it?

James 1:5–8; 3:13, 17–18

2 Timothy 3:14–17

WORD WEALTH

Proverbs describes God as a shield and buckler to the righteous, to those people who put their trust in Him (Prov. 2:7; 30:5). Hebrew has several words to describe shields such as *shelet*, a small shield, and *tsinnah*, the large shield that covers much of the soldier. Neither of these words is used in Proverbs; the shield here is the buckler (*meginnah*),[5] a "small round shield held by a handle at arm's length," which can fight off individual blows from an enemy.[6] God is called a buckler for His people; a shield who wards off enemy blows.

The shield in Ephesians 6:16 (the shield of faith that quenches all the fiery darts of the wicked one) was a large, door-shaped, oblong shield,[7] which protects most of the body, similar to the *tsinnah*. Shields were made of leather, brass, or copper stretched over or attached to wooden frames. The metal shields often looked red in the sunlight.[8]

WISDOM'S REWARDS (2:1–22; 4:1–27)

The greatest reward that comes from wisdom is the fear and knowledge of God (Prov. 2:5). Wisdom, then, is vitally connected with knowing God and having a proper relationship with Him.

How do we receive wisdom? (Prov. 2:6)

How does wisdom help us? (Prov. 2:7, 8)

What else do we have if we have wisdom first? (Prov. 2:9)

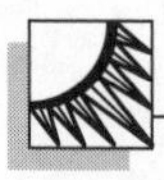

FAITH ALIVE

The Scripture tells us God will bless us exceedingly if we seek wisdom. The Lord Jesus told us something similar in Matthew 6:33, that if we seek the rule of God over our lives and His righteousness, His ways to do rightly, all the things of this life and the next that we need He will provide.

1. From the following verses, name some ways we can yield to God's rule over us.

Proverbs 3:5–8

Proverbs 3:9–10

Proverbs 3:11–12

2. Pray for the Spirit of Wisdom to identify anything in your life that needs to be changed so that all your ways will be right before God.

If we do not seek wisdom, and we reject God's right ways to live, what problems will we have?

Proverbs 2:13–22

Proverbs 4:14–19

Proverbs 5:1–23

Proverbs 6:20—7:27

When we obey the wisdom of God, what benefits do we receive?

Proverbs 4:7–9

Proverbs 4:10–13

Proverbs 4:22

Proverbs 2:12–20

Word Wealth

The word "crown" in Proverbs 4:9 is used as a symbol of victory, reward, and honor. The word in Hebrew, *'atarah*, refers to a headpiece of great beauty that signifies command or superiority, as in a king or ruler. Another word, *nehzer*, is translated "crown" but means something set apart or consecrated, like the dedicated hair of the Nazarite (see Prov. 27:24; Zech. 9:16).[9]

Look up the following passages and summarize what each says about the *spiritual* meanings of "crown."

Isaiah 28:5

Revelation 19:12

Proverbs 12:4

Proverbs 17:6

Proverbs 20:29

Spiritual Wisdom (3:1–35)

We have seen that the greatest blessing wisdom brings is the knowledge of God. Now we hear from Solomon that the greatest wisdom is spiritual, focused on God Himself. What benefits does this wisdom give us?

Proverbs 3:1, 2

Proverbs 3:4

How do we become spiritually wise? (Prov. 3:5–9)

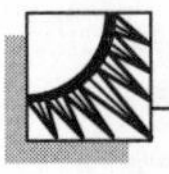

FAITH ALIVE

Read the following passages and write down ways you can trust God completely with things in your life.

Psalm 115:8

Proverbs 11:28

Proverbs 16:20

Proverbs 28:26

We also become spiritually wise by accepting discipline from the Lord.

Why does He discipline us? (Prov. 3:11–12)

Too often, we are ready to blame the devil, or the church, or Aunt Ramona, or someone else when trials or difficulties come our way. It may be that God is using these problems (which we have created for ourselves because we have strayed from His ways) to teach us and correct us.

BIBLE EXTRA

Read the following passages, and relate for each how God used a life situation to train a biblical character.

Genesis 40:1–23

Numbers 22:15–34

Ruth 1:1–22

Daniel 1:1–21

WORD WEALTH

In Proverbs 5:4, the young son is warned to stay away from the immoral, adulterous woman because, though she looked good, in the end "she is bitter as wormwood . . . ."

Wormwood (the Hebrew word is *la'anah*) is a plant found in the Middle East, known for its extreme bitterness to taste. The word is used with other similarly repulsive terms such as gall and hemlock (Deut. 29:18; Amos 5:7; 6:12).[10] Wormwood is used in the Book of Revelation to refer to a great star that fell from heaven and struck the earth, producing water so bitter that people died from drinking it (Rev. 8:10, 11). An old folk tradition attributes the existence of the plant, wormwood, to a time when the serpent, Satan, slithered out of Eden, and the plant sprang to life on his path.[11] Legend aside, a cloying bitterness is what awaits those ensnared in immorality.

Christians are called by God to live righteous, holy lives of responsible, wise behavior. Foolishness, crime, and adultery not only destroy our witness to the world but will also destroy our lives. By trusting God with all the situations of life and responding positively to His correction, we will be greatly blessed and be able to bless others as well.

1. James Strong, *New Strong's™ Exhaustive Concordance* (Nashville: Thomas Nelson, 1984), "Dictionary of the Hebrew Bible," #1175, #39.
2. Samuel Fallows, *The Popular and Critical Bible Encyclopedia and Scriptural Dictionary,* (Chicago: Howard-Severance Co., 1916), 1728.
3. Strong, #116.
4. Fallows, 1728.
5. Fallows, 1576.
6. *Merriam-Webster's New Collegiate® Dictionary*, Tenth Edition © 1996 by Merriam-Webster Inc.
7. Fallows, 1577.
8. Ibid.
9. Ibid.
10. Ibid., 1735.
11. E. Cobham Brewer, *Dictionary of Phrase and Fable* (Philadelphia: J.B. Lippincott Co., 1894), 1313.

Lesson 3/The Righteous Way (10:1—12:28)

John was a businessman who tried every way he knew to be successful. At first, he followed the advice of his friends and fellow business people. He worked 12 hours a day, hired his employees for as little as he could, and took every shortcut. His business didn't "go under," but success was such a struggle.

One day John came to know the Lord Jesus Christ and got a new perspective on life. Now, he realized, his business, as well as everything in his life, had a new boss—God. He wondered if God would handle the business differently; business is still business, you know. As John searched the Scriptures and began to learn how to live the Christian life, he realized things had to be changed at work.

First, John reduced the work hours so he and his employees could spend more time with their families. Then he raised all the salaries to their appropriate levels. Then he insured that every product and service were top quality. The results were amazing!

He and his employees became happier, more productive people. They still faced challenges, but the new atmosphere and attitude helped everyone work out the problems better. Customers appreciated the company's products and service, and sales went up. Success had actually come more easily and John's life was more meaningful as he looked for ways to use his success to help his church and community.

John's story is a good example of how God helps us live the abundant life. Many people seek shortcuts to success; they often take advantage of others and bring all kinds of trouble upon themselves. But the only way to live a truly good life, one with health, integrity, and respect, is by speaking and doing what is right, according to God's definition. You may not receive the acceptance of the world, but you will receive the blessing of God.

Word Wealth

The word "blessing" used several times in Proverbs is *berakah*, a benediction (to speak well of), a promise of prosperity, the opposite of a curse.[1]

What does Proverbs 10:22 teach about blessing?

How does a community receive God's blessing? (Prov. 11:11)

How does a business person receive God's blessing? (Prov. 11:26)

To receive God's blessing, how should we respond to wickedness in our world? (Prov. 24:25)

The idea of blessing can be understood in one of four ways. First, the patriarchs and leaders of Israel blessed their sons and younger generations to bestow on them certain privileges, responsibilities, and wealth (see Gen. 27).

Also, blessings are good things given by God which bring happiness (see Deut. 28:8). A third concept of blessing is the "invocation of God's favor upon a person" (see Gen. 27:12). Finally, a gift is also a blessing (see Josh. 25:19).[2]

BIBLE EXTRA

Look up the following New Testament passages and tell the meaning of "blessing" in each one.

Luke 24:53

Galatians 3:14

James 3:10

Revelation 5:12, 13

What is similar among these occurrences of "blessing"?

In what ways do these occurrences express different nuances of meaning for "blessing"?

How are these New Testament examples of blessing similar to or different from the Old Testament meanings?

RIGHTEOUS WORDS (10:1–32)

Proverbs highlights the importance of words, especially spoken ones. The Bible reveals to us that words are not just empty vibrations floating through the air. They have power and meaning. They go forth to accomplish things (Is. 9:8; 45:23; 55:11). They possess a strange and wonderful power, which many modern people do not realize. They cannot be "taken back" or replaced. Once spoken, words affect other people, and they reveal the heart and soul of the person who speaks them (Matt. 12:34; 15:11, 18; James 3:8–12).

BIBLE EXTRA

Read the following passages and note the power and purpose of speaking words.

Joshua 6:10–20

2 Chronicles 6:10, 17

Psalm 105:19

Jeremiah 1:12

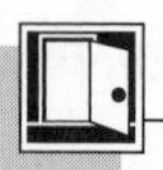

BEHIND THE SCENES

Many proverbs deal with harvest time. Harvest in ancient Israel occurred twice a year, first as a barley harvest in the valleys, in April after the rainy season (Prov. 26:1). The wheat harvest of the highlands often continued into June, a hot season (Prov. 25:13). Great festivals and spiritual thanksgiving feasts were held at the close of the harvest (see Lev. 23:6, 10–14). The Book of Ruth is a beautiful story that involves the activities of harvest time.

What do the wise persons do at harvest? (Prov. 10:5)

What do the foolish people do at harvest? (Prov. 10:5)[3]

Proverbs 10 reveals that good words from righteous people are great blessings. What does Proverbs 10:11 teach about good words?

What do good words provide? (Prov. 10:13)

How do good words bless people? (Prov. 10:21)

One of the classic proverbs about words (10:19), says that too much talk always leads to sin, so the wise person doesn't say much. Abraham Lincoln is credited with a memorable paraphrase of this proverb, "Better to be silent and thought a fool, than to open your mouth and remove all doubt."

Righteous Deeds (11:1–31)

The wise person does good deeds that demonstrate righteous character. Proverbs 11 mentions many examples of such people. Read the following passages and answer the questions.

How do the righteous conduct business? (Prov. 11:1, 3, 15)

What do the righteous do about the poor? (Prov. 11:24, 25)

What do the righteous do with secrets and important information? (Prov. 11:12–14)

Specifically mentioned are righteous women; gracious women who are honorable (11:16). What does Proverbs say about women who are immodest or irresponsible (see Prov. 11:22)?

The Lord expects His people to exhibit godliness, to do good things, and be recognized as people whose good lives come from His indwelling Spirit (Matt. 5:13–16; Gal. 5:22–25; James 2:14–17).

WORD WEALTH

Generally, the Old Testament warns us against taking on or insuring another person's debts, an act called *surety*. Proverbs particularly paints a terrible picture of this idea. In Proverbs 11:15, suffering awaits anyone who is surety for a stranger. The advice of the wise sages is never to let yourself get in such a position. To be a surety, usually you would have to pay a security bond, a deposit of money, to guarantee that the other person would pay his debts. The Hebrew word for surety is *'awrab*, which means "to braid."[4]

This word paints a clear picture of the problem. Two people are "braided" together as one so that the debts of one become the debts of both. This picture takes on special meaning for us when we realize that the Lord Jesus Christ is our *surety* (Heb. 7:22), guaranteeing the blessings of the new covenant.

Read the following passages and write out reasons why being a personal surety for someone's debts is not a wise thing to do.

Proverbs 6:1

Proverbs 17:18

Proverbs 20:16

Proverbs 22:26

Righteous Results (12:1–28)

If we speak and do righteous things because the fruit of the Spirit flows from us, then good things happen as a result. Read the following passages and list the good things.

Proverbs 12:2

Proverbs 12:7

Proverbs 12:8

Proverbs 12:13, 14

Bible Extra

God delights in us (Prov. 12:22), and we will live abundantly (12:28), which is God's intent for His children. He wants to bless us greatly and make us examples of His grace and love. Our part is to love Him, obey Him, and live according to His ways. Read the following passages and answer the questions.

Exodus 15:23–26

What are we supposed to do?

What will God do?

Deuteronomy 7:12–15
What are we supposed to do?

What will God do?

1 John 2:3–6
What are we supposed to do?

What will be the result?

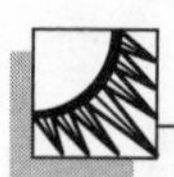

FAITH ALIVE

Clearly, God is interested in righteousness. He is holy and hates sin. He wants to protect us and provide for us in this life as well as the life to come.

What has God done to help us live righteous lives?

1 Corinthians 10:13

2 Peter 1:3, 4

Exodus 19:5

Colossians 1:9–14

Romans 5:1–5

1. James Strong, *New Strong's™ Exhaustive Concordance* (Nashville: Thomas Nelson, 1984), "Dictionary to the Hebrew Bible," #1293.

2. Samuel Fallows, *The Popular and Critical Bible Encyclopedia and Scriptural Dictionary,* (Chicago: Howard Severance Co., 1916), 292–293.

3. Fallows, 766, who refers to J. D. Davis, *Dictionary of the Bible,* (Grand Rapids, MI: Baker, 1978), which includes the biblical references for the feasts (872–873).

4. Fallows, 1621.

Lesson 4/The Sensible Way
(13:1—15:33)

There is the old story about a couple who were expecting their first child. All the proper preparations were made and their son was born without a hitch. They were delirious with joy.

The baby grew quickly and did all the things that babies do, except he never spoke. Not one word. The parents had him checked by numerous doctors, who all said that he was perfectly normal. They couldn't understand why he never said anything.

The boy continued to grow normally but he never responded to any of the attempts his parents made to get him to talk. One day, when the boy was about eight years old, the family sat down to a dinner of soup and sandwiches. The boy tasted the soup and exclaimed, "Oh, this soup is terrible!"

The parents both shouted for joy! Their son *could* talk and *did* talk for the first time! "Why haven't you said anything all these years?" they inquired.

"Well, everything was just fine, 'til now," he replied.

In different ways, this story illustrates two of the many truths taught in Proverbs. The boy certainly guarded his mouth (Prov. 13:3) but he didn't behave sensibly because he didn't carry on normal conversation with his parents.

Proverbs 13—15 instructs us in ways to behave sensibly. Lesson 3 taught us the value of righteousness. Now we learn the benefits of common sense, sensible ways.

Sensible Instruction (13:1–25)

The purpose of the Book of Proverbs is instruction, teaching us how to conduct our lives. Read the following passages and describe what happens (1) when we behave sensibly, and (2) what happens if we behave foolishly.

Proverbs 13:1, 15

(1)

(2)

Proverbs 13:4

(1)

(2)

Proverbs 13:7, 8

(1)

(2)

Proverbs 13:17

(1)

(2)

Proverbs 13:18

(1)

(2)

Bible Extra

Proverbs 13:22 mentions an inheritance left by a good man, even to his posterity of the third generation. A basic principle of the Old Testament regarding inheritance is the "double portion" (Deut. 21:17; 2 Kin. 2:9). The double portion usually went to the eldest son, and the other sons received single portions of father's estate. These would be the portions for three sons:

A	A	B	C

The eldest son (A) receives the double portion, or two shares, and the other brothers receive one share apiece. "Double portion" does not mean twice what the father had.

Read the following passages and name the inheritance given and to whom.

Numbers 18:20

Numbers 27:1–11

Ephesians 1:11

Ephesians 1:14, 18

1 Peter 1:4

WORD WEALTH

Proverbs tells us "a scoffer does not listen to rebuke" (Prov. 13:1). Who is the scoffer? Read the following passages and describe the scoffer.

Proverbs 14:6

Proverbs 15:12

Proverbs 19:28

Proverbs 21:24

Proverbs 22:10

BIBLE EXTRA

Scoffers, or scorners, show contempt for someone or something by mocking, ridiculing, or otherwise acting disrespectfully.[1]

How does Peter describe scoffers? (2 Pet. 3:3–5)

How does the Apostle Paul describe the scoffers of the last days? (2 Tim. 3:1–9)

Sensible Action (14:1–35)

After we receive instruction about how to behave sensibly, we must actually act that way. What ways does Proverbs 14 tell us to act?

Proverbs 14:1

Proverbs 14:7

Proverbs 14:15

Proverbs 14:21

Proverbs 14:23

Behind the Scenes

Oxen (Prov. 14:4) are domesticated cattle, which were used in many ways by the ancient Hebrews.[2] Besides carrying heavy burdens and providing milk products and meat, oxen provided the power for plowing fields.

What does the Old Testament teach about how the farmer should treat the ox? (Deut. 25:4) What does the New Testament teach, using this same Old Testament law, about how we should treat people?

1 Corinthians 9:9

1 Timothy 5:18

The saying in Proverbs 14:4 teaches that, though oxen are messy, we gain much more for our trouble by having them around. What modern examples of this truth can you think of?

The picture of oxen is used symbolically and spiritually in the Scriptures to illustrate deep truths. Read the following passages and describe the truths that oxen illustrate.

Numbers 22:4

Proverbs 7:22

Proverbs 25:17

Jeremiah 11:19[3]

WORD WEALTH

A "backslider" is full of selfishness and seeks to satisfy his life with earthly, temporary treasures (Prov. 14:14). To backslide means to "gradually, voluntarily, and insensibly" turn from the truth and knowledge of God and return to godless, sinful living.[4]

Describe the situation and how backsliding affects people in the following passages.

Hosea 11:7

Acts 21:21

1 Timothy 4:1

2 Thessalonians 2:3

SENSIBLE RESULTS (15:1–33)

After we have received sensible instruction (Prov. 13) and put it into practice (Prov. 14), we find that such a lifestyle pleases God and produces a successful and happy life.

What actions keep relationships pleasant? (Prov. 15:1, 2)

How does a scoffer live his life? (Prov. 15:12)

What condition of our souls is seen on our faces? (Prov. 15:13)

What is life like for a happy person? (Prov. 15:15)

Proverbs 15 also teaches us how God deals with different kinds of people.

How does God feel when righteous people pray? (Prov. 15:8, 9)

What does He do when we pray? (Prov. 15:29)

How does God feel when we seek righteousness? (Prov. 15:9)

How does God keep in touch with the lives of people? (Prov. 15:3, 11)

What will God do to the wicked? (Prov. 15:25)

What will God do for the innocent? (Prov. 15:25)

What pleases God? (Prov. 15:26, 33)

WORD WEALTH

Hell and destruction are mentioned in Proverbs 15:11 as things not hidden from God's sight. Hell in this passage is ***sheol***, the world of the dead, a place where the spirits of the dead reside.[5] The Bible teaches us that everlasting life is more than an eternal existence of a spirit without a body; it is also resurrection of the body and eternal, full, abundant life in the presence of God (1 Cor. 15:12–20; Rev. 20:11–14; 21:1–4). Destruction, in Proverbs 15:11, is the Hebrew word ***abaddon***, which means corruption, decay, or decomposition.[6]

Who will bear the name Abaddon at the time of the Lord's second coming? (Rev. 9:11)

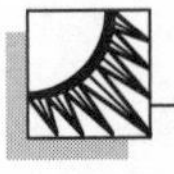

FAITH ALIVE

We think that behaving righteously is hard to do consistently. Sometimes we don't want to be kind or fair or sensible. What help do the Scriptures give us?

What relationship to sin do believers have? (Rom. 6:6–11)

What do we do to keep sin from ruling us? (Rom. 6:12–18)

How can we conquer temptations? (1 Cor. 10:13)

What makes us capable of living godly lives? (1 Cor. 1:3–9; 12:4–11)

What results flow from our lives when we yield ourselves to the Spirit? (Gal. 5:22–25)

1. *Merriam-Webster's Collegiate® Dictionary*, Tenth Edition © 1996 by Merriam-Webster Inc.

2. Samuel Fallows, *The Popular and Critical Bible Encyclopedia and Scriptural Dictionary* (Chicago: Howard-Severance Co., 1916), 1270.

3. Fallows, 1270.

4. Fallows, 219.

5. James Strong, *New Strong's™ Exhaustive Concordance* (Nashville: Thomas Nelson, 1984), "Dictionary to the Hebrew Bible," #111.

6. Strong, #7.

Lesson 5/The Honorable Way
(16:1—18:24)

The following bloopers actually appeared in church bulletins or newsletters. Read them and enjoy:

For those of you who have children and don't know it, we have a nursery in the basement.

Lot's wife was a pillar of salt by day and a ball of fire by night.

The pastor's massage begins at 11:00, followed by sinning at 11:35.

The fifth commandment is humor your father and mother.

These unplanned "slips of the tongue" (or keyboard!) illustrate how easy it is for us to blunder with our speech, even when we have good intentions. Proverbs 16—18 teaches us the honorable way to abundant living which includes not only our behavior, but also our motives and our speech.

Honorable Motives (16:1–33)

God looks on the heart, the inner intentions and motives, as well as on our actions. He is very concerned about the foundation upon which all our lives are built—the condition of our inner person.

What does Jesus say about our motives? (Matt. 5:27, 28; 6:1–4)

What does the heart, the inner person, have to do for a person to be saved? (Rom. 10:9, 10)

How does God want us to live? (Eph. 6:6–8)

Proverbs 16 tells us much about God's character and care for us. The Lord is sovereign, the ruler of the history of humanity (Dan. 5:18–24). For each verse, write what it says about God's purpose for humanity and His activity toward people.

Proverbs 16:4

Proverbs 16:5

Proverbs 16:9

How does God judge our hearts?
Proverbs 16:2

Proverbs 16:3

Proverbs 16:5

WORD WEALTH

In Proverbs 16:3, the word rendered "commit" is the Hebrew word *galal,* meaning "to roll, roll down, roll away, remove." In this text, the reader is encouraged to roll his works into God's care. The picture is of a camel, burdened with a heavy load; when the load is to be removed, the camel kneels down, tilts far to one side, and the load rolls off.

What good benefits do we receive by living with good motives?

Proverbs 16:7

Proverbs 16:9

Proverbs 16:20

WORD WEALTH

"Divination is on the lips of the king / His mouth must not transgress in judgment" (Prov. 16:10). The term *divination* can be confusing here. Usually the word is the Hebrew *qacam*, which means to determine by lot or provide information through magic or witchcraft.[1]

Clearly here in Proverbs 16, though, the king is not a magician but a ruler responsible to give judgment by divine guidance, inspired by the Lord to render just and fair judgment.

Honorable Behavior (17:1–28)

If our hearts and motives are right before God, then our behavior will be godly. Proverbs 17 contrasts this good behavior with the bad conduct of people whose motives are selfish. Read the following passages and describe the actions God rejects, as well as the opposite action He approves.

Proverbs 17:1
God rejects:

God accepts:

Proverbs 17:4
God rejects:

God accepts:

Proverbs 17:5
God rejects:

God accepts:

Proverbs 17:15
God rejects:

God accepts:

Proverbs 17:20

God rejects:

God accepts:

The wise sages of Israel knew the nature of people, both good and evil, and what conduct best suits a person in the family of God.

Why does God test our hearts? (Prov. 17:3; 1 Pet. 1:6–9)

How do we help a friend who has personal troubles? (Prov. 17:9, 10)

What happens to us if we do evil things to others? (Prov. 17:13)

How do we keep quarrels from happening? (Prov. 17:14; 4:1–10)

Word Wealth

Proverbs 17:3 describes the process of refining metals, through fire and heat, straining out the impurities. The refiners sat and watched the melting process so that, when they saw their own reflections in the liquid metal, they knew the impurities had been removed. After the metal is melted and purified, it is poured into molds to make expensive jewelry, decorations, or implements.[2]

The term *refiner* is used figuratively in many places in the Scripture. Describe what refiner or refining means in the following passages.

Psalm 119:140

Isaiah 48:10

Zechariah 13:7

Malachi 3:2, 3

1 Peter 1:22

WORD WEALTH

Friend. *re'a.* Alternately: companion, neighbor, fellowman; a familiar person. This noun occurs in the Bible more than 180 times. Its use in Proverbs 17:17 is a prescription for a healthy friendship: a friend should love at all times. The responsibility to one's neighbor (using the same Hebrew word) is outlined in Psalm 101:5; Proverbs 24:28; and Zechariah 8:17.

GOD'S BEST FOR US

One day, when my eldest son was about three years old, he noticed his mother cooking rice on the stove. He was hungry (always was and still is at age 20) and began to vigorously demonstrate his feelings to his mom. He jumped and cried, insisting on a bite of rice. Now his mother could have given him the undone, hard, tasteless rice at his demand, but obviously he would not have appreciated such a gift; besides, rice in that state was not really what he wanted. So she made him wait until the rice was fully cooked, prepared perfectly to satisfy his need and desire. In the meantime, he created his own stress, worry, heartache, and discomfort, none of which were necessary nor intended from the cook and parent. He caused himself all his trouble.

So we, too, cause ourselves most of our troubles in an effort to control outcomes, times, results, goals, and other events of life. We have so little patience and much less faith. Faith requires trust. We trust Jesus to do the best for us—even when (and especially when) the circumstances do not look to us like what we would have wanted.

We must meet all things in life with the idea that either He has sent them or He will use them for our good. If the event is indeed evil, God's wisdom is available to help us discern how to respond, how to resist the evil with good. But God will use even evil to demonstrate His love and power, as He did in the Exodus, when the Israelites were trapped at the Red Sea, or in Luke with the man who was born blind. Often we interpret events only as evil when God intends to use them to produce discipline or stronger faith (James 1:2–4).

WORD WEALTH

Instruction, *Musar* comes from the verb *yasar,* "to reform, chastise, discipline, instruct." *Musar* appears fifty times in the Old Testament, thirty of these in Proverbs. *Musar* is broad enough to encompass chastening by words and by punishments (Prov. 1:3; 22:15). Isaiah 53:5 states, "The chastisement for our peace was upon Him, and by His stripes we are healed." In Proverbs 3:11, we are urged not to "despise the chastening of the LORD." nor to grow weary of His correction. A wicked man may even "die for lack of instruction" (Prov. 5:23). Thus *musar* includes all forms of discipline intended to lead to a transformed life.[3]

HONORABLE SPEECH (18:1–24)

Our speech, the things we say, will reflect what is in our hearts (Matt. 12:34). Good words, spoken from a pure heart, are blessings to everyone and do much to glorify God.

What does Proverbs 18 teach us about good speech?
18:4

18:21

What does Proverbs 18 teach us about bad speech?
18:2

18:6

18:7

18:8

18:13

BIBLE EXTRA

"The name of the Lord is a strong tower; the righteous run to it and are safe" (Prov. 18:10). Names, to the ancient Hebrews and many other cultures, had significant meanings, such as Jesus, "the Lord saves" (Matt. 1:21). To use someone's name was to represent that person as if he or she were actually there in person (see John 14:13, 14; Col. 3:17).

Read the following passages and tell how the name of God or Jesus describes something of His character.

Psalm 8:1, 9

Psalm 20:1, 7

Acts 9:15

Philippians 2:9, 10

Revelation 19:16

Behind the Scenes

Proverbs 18:16 is often misunderstood. The verse says that "a man's gift makes room for him," which sometimes is taken to mean that whatever talents, abilities, or spiritual gifts someone has will force opportunities to arise so those abilities can be used. In the context of this passage in Proverbs 18, the second part of the verse helps us understand the saying," . . . and brings him before great men." The proverb reveals the old custom that when a person wanted to contact a ruler or other person of higher social or spiritual rank, he or she would bring a gift to the person. People in the Old Testament followed this custom when they wished to hear from a prophet of God (see 1 Sam. 9:6–10).

Read the following passages and tell who gave the gift and for what purpose.

Numbers 8:19

Proverbs 21:14

Matthew 2:11

Matthew 5:23, 24

Acts 2:38; 1:8

FAITH ALIVE

The use of words in speech is a mighty force whether we preach the gospel, command a demon to depart, or criticize another person. How should we speak, and how can we be sure to speak honorably? Write what help each Scripture offers.

Psalm 34:11–14

Psalm 141:3

Proverbs 21:23

James 1:26, 27

James 3:5–13

1. James Strong, *New Strong's™ Exhaustive Concordance* (Nashville: Thomas Nelson, 1984), "Dictionary to the Hebrew Bible," #104.

2. Samuel Fallows, *The Popular and Critical Bible Encyclopedia and Scriptural Dictionary* (Chicago: Howard-Severance Co., 1916), 1435.

3. Jack Hayford (Gen. Ed.), *Hayford's Bible Handbook* (Nashville: Thomas Nelson, 1995), 656.

Lesson 6/The Disciplined Way
(19:1—22:16)

"Hold him, Jim!" screamed Harry. The horse was wild, jumping and bumping all over the corral.

"I don't think I can," returned Jim. "He's got a burr in his saddle or something." The explanation seemed feeble. This horse was just plain wild and wouldn't be tamed. He wanted nothing better than to kick our heads in.

"Hurry, Jim, get this harness over his nose." Harry grabbed the stallion around the neck and pulled his head hard toward the ground. The horse twitched and writhed furiously, but Harry held on. Jim barely got the harness on when Harry's strength gave way. But now the wild horse was caught, held by the harness so the cowboys could break his rebellion.

This little story recalls a western scene, the breaking of a wild horse. Such an animal was useless to the cowboys because he was so uncooperative and uncontrollable. He needed discipline.

So do we.

Without training, which involves enforcing obedience, we would also be uncooperative toward God and selfish, doing our own things, going our own ways.

God is in the training business because, without Him, we can do nothing (John 15:50). He wants us fit for service, lean-and-mean ministry machines. So He trains us, disciplines us. Proverbs 19:1—22:16 is one of those parts of the Word that best helps us get our practical training. We'll look at this section topically, focusing on certain passages that emphasize first, the individual, then the family, and finally, the community.

Word Wealth

In Proverbs 19:6, the phrase "entreat the favor of" involves human relationships. The only other places where this same context appears is Job 11:19 and Psalm 45:12. Usually the phrase is religious and concerns prayer to God, "entreating His favor" for some request. In Eastern tradition, a person of lower social rank must approach a person of higher social rank with gifts, to "entreat his favor" (literally to "smooth his face" in the Hebrew). The sacrifice in worship is a picture of this behavior in the religious context.

In this proverb, the process is applied to a person who wishes to entreat the favor of a ruler or socially superior person, and who therefore gives gifts for friendship.[1] The same idea is expressed in an often misinterpreted proverb (18:16) that simply explains that the gift to the superior effectively achieves its purpose, to gain his favor. This behavior is not bribery; the biblical concept of bribery is a secret payoff to get one person with power to unjustly judge for your advantage over another person whose case should be judged in his favor.

The Disciplined Person

Proverbs 19 indicates several ways a person may be disciplined. How does verse 8 say we can be disciplined?

What two ways of discipline are indicated in vv. 15 and 16?

Responses to bad behavior appear in vv. 18, 19, and 25. What are they, and how do these responses discipline us?

What is another way we are disciplined? (see v. 20)

All of these ways stretch, test, and strain us to some extent. That is the part of discipline some people dislike because it is not comfortable. Learning a trade, a skill, or sport takes time and effort, and often a person has to shake off failures with a determination to rise up triumphantly.

Hard work is physically, emotionally, and mentally draining, but it is rewarding and satisfying, like making a good grade in school. God's laws do not always accommodate us. They certainly do not let us "feed our flesh" with selfish behavior, but they mold our "wants" so we desire to do God's will, which always turns out to be the best for us.

WORD WEALTH

The term "buries" his hand in the dish (Prov. 19:24) means to conceal or hide. The hand is used because the modern knife, fork, and spoon were not used at that time, even for soup (see Judg. 6:19).[2] This proverb is humorously overstated. We can picture the lazy man stuffing his whole hand, with great display of fatigue no doubt, into the bowl. His hand is completely covered, and he does not have the strength even to lift it up to his mouth to eat.

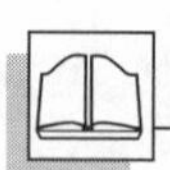

BIBLE EXTRA

Look up the following passages and summarize what each says about discipline.

Proverbs 9:7–9

Nehemiah 4:6

Ephesians 4:28

Discipline produces strength of character, the ability to be responsible, honest, and dependable with integrity and righteousness (see James 1:2–4, 5:10, 11; 1 Pet. 1:6, 7, 22). From people of such character, strong families are built.

WORD WEALTH

A worthless person is often called in Scripture a "son of Belial." In Proverbs 19:28, a disreputable witness is a "witness of Belial" in the Hebrew language. Actually, this name is the worst thing you could call someone in Hebrew. Such a person is a complete rebel, disobedient, uncontrollable, you-name-it bad person. In the New Testament, the term is clearly associated with Satan, so that such a person is a "son of Satan," the lowest form of evil.[3] Look in Judges 19:22; 1 Samuel 2:12; 2 Samuel 16:7; 1 Kings 21:10; and 2 Corinthians 6:15 for other references to this term.

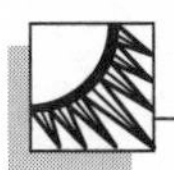

FAITH ALIVE

What kind of discipline have you experienced?

How has it benefited you?

How can you now see God at work in the situation?

THE DISCIPLINED FAMILY

Families are the basic social units of society. As families go, so go society and the world. Modern industrialized societies emphasize the individual more than the family. We end up with individualistic expressions, such as "do your own thing; be completely independent; you don't need anyone else." Many families are so broken that the individual members are driven from each other. Counseling ministries have greatly increased lately, especially marriage and family specialists, because of this modern social disaster.

Christians are called to produce strong families, through whom the ministry of God's mercy and love pours forth to a hurting world.

BIBLE EXTRA

Look up the following passages and summarize the ways Christian families can minister in the world.

Ephesians 3:15

1 Timothy 5:4, 8

Exodus 12:26, 27

God works greatly in strong Christian families, using them as examples of righteousness and godliness to the world and blessing to the church.

Behind the Scenes

Notice in Scripture, especially in Proverbs, three views about *poverty.* First, some people became poor by misfortune or disaster, which was beyond their control. These people should be helped by those who have wealth. In fact, by giving to these poor, we give to God, and He will bless us (Prov. 19:17). A second view in Proverbs is that a person is better poor than wicked and rich (Prov. 19:22). The unjust, deceitful gain of riches is a curse which results in bad things for such a foolish person (Prov. 20:17, 21, 23).

Finally, there is the person who is poor because of laziness and foolishness. He has all the potential and opportunity to do right and be successful, but he causes his own destruction by his folly. Such a person has few friends (Prov. 19:4); even his family has no use for him (Prov. 19:7).

Look up the following passages and answer the questions.

What will happen to us if we neglect the misfortunate poor? (Prov. 21:13)

What does Proverbs 21:6–8 say about rich people who are also wicked?

How did the lazy man become poor? (Prov. 20:4, 13)

What will happen to the lazy poor person? (Prov. 19:15, 24)

Chapter 20 of Proverbs reveals several ideals that families should experience.

What does v. 6 say about relationships among family members?

What kind of father, mentioned in v. 7, is a blessing to his children?

What does v. 11 teach about a child's reputation?

How should children treat adults (see vv. 20 and 29)?

PROBING THE DEPTHS

One of the major themes of Proverbs is family relationships. The book provides teaching for the husband, the wife, the relationship between them, and the children. What kind of experience should marriage be, according to these passages from Proverbs?

18:22

19:14

31:10–12, 28–31

How should marriage partners treat each other?
31:10–12

31:27–29

What kinds of behavior cause problems in a marriage?
19:13

21:9, 19

25:24

What does Proverbs teach about training children?
20:11

22:6, 15

23:13, 14

29:15, 17

Consider the Children

Children are offspring; chips off the old block, so we say. But adults who have been taught to stifle and shut out any childishness, may consider children inferior creatures, like dogs and cats, to be ruled or pampered, or made in the image of Dad or Mom. These adults insist that children act like "all good natured adults" should, live without error, know everything they are supposed to know and do everything right, so that parents will not be embarrassed by them. Right away the situation is lost because children are real people with real personalities, needs, and desires of their own. They are neither playthings in a cherished dream of long ago nor enlisted soldiers serving to please their royal magistrates.

Children are people—growing people, certainly, but full-fledged members of the human race. Remember the Lord Jesus Christ valued and loved them immensely. At least one child served as an example to the "grown-up" disciples that childlikeness is a necessary prerequisite to participation in God's kingdom (Mark 10:13–16). Consider the qualities of childlikeness exalted by Christ as qualities we all have but seldom use.

Childlikeness means pure faith, joy of discovery, thirst for adventure and challenge, tender trust, honest emotion, and growth. Faith in children is so simple and profound. They can believe all sorts of fantastic things; "impossible" is not in their vocabularies. Because their imaginations are not easily squelched, children have no trouble moving from the world of play, fairies, space invaders, and dolls to the realities of bath, supper, clothes, and nap. In fact, the healthiest, most creative people come from childhoods where imaginative exercises have been encouraged and developed.

Children are real people; we should never underestimate their inteligence nor their capabilities. We should also not overestimate their adaptability or their self-sufficiency; they really have the same needs and desires that all of us do, put in simpler packages. Children are people—only smaller, only newer, only fresher, only simpler. The mission of adults is to train these younger people, educate them to the best and highest of God's gifts of life, show them the way to live, and guide them as they search for their places in the world. For this mission, every parent needs all the wisdom God provides in Proverbs and in the rest of His word.

No theme is more likely to touch God's heart than that which is capturing the renewed attention of every sensitive Spirit-filled person today: The Priority of the Family. As redeemed souls walk in renewed relationship with God through Christ, it is consistent with the whole of Scripture that they prioritize their learning of the biblical pathway to fulfilling and divinely ordered family living.

The Bible unfolds its story with a dual display of health in family relationships. Most obviously, the first pair (Adam and Eve) are at peace, in union, and experiencing the perfect intention of God's creative design as the "two shall be made one" married realtionship. But another family is clearly present, as God—the heavenly Father of all earth and heaven's family (Eph. 3:14–15)—is seen in His foundational role as Giver, Nourisher, Protector of mankind's destiny.

Review each of the following passages, and write for each the principle it conveys to help make your home more like the way God intended it to be.

Genesis 1:26–28

Ephesians 3:14–15

1 Corinthians 11:3

Ephesians 5:22–33

1 Peter 3:1–7

Colossians 3:18–19, 23–24

Hosea 2:16–17, 19–20

1 Corinthians 7:3–4

Isaiah 54:5

Malachi 2:13–14, 16

Matthew 19:1–9

Psalm 68:5–6

Hosea 11:1, 3–4

Psalm 127:3–5

Ephesians 6:4

Proverbs 13:24

Romans 15:5–7

The Disciplined Society

Societies are built from families, which are built from individual members. The chain is only as strong as each link, so societies begin to crumble if the family and individual links weaken. We have seen how the individual can be disciplined and receive the personal benefits. The family that is built from spiritually strong individuals also produces blessing for society. Let us see how disciplined societies produce blessing for the world.

What does Proverbs 21:1 teach about God's role in the governing of societies? (also see Dan. 5:18–30)

What happens when rulers obey God? (Prov. 21:3)

What happens when rulers resist God? (see vv. 4–8)

Behind the Scenes

Proverbs 20:14 describes a scene which may sound strange to modern people who shop in grocery stores and malls where prices for items are clearly marked. The marketplace of the Middle East, especially in biblical times, thrived on "horse-trading" or bargaining for a selling price. In this passage, the customer has continually complained that the price is too high, but when the customer leaves the market, he brags to friends about the great bargain he obtained. Either the customer was a shrewd bargainer and got the seller to come far down on the price or the customer wants his friends to think so.

Read Genesis 23 for a beautiful description of a bargaining match between Abraham and Ephron the Hittite. The conversation has to be read with a little tongue-in-cheek humor because Ephron appears at first glance to offer his field to Abraham as a gift. But continue the story to find that this conversation is simply the bargaining method of the people of that culture. It is a wonderful example.

Wickedness in society adversely affects everyone (Prov. 21:10), so we Christians cannot ignore the rest of the world. We have to take a stand for righteousness, which should bring blessing to all but the wicked (Prov. 21:15). The church must care about social justice, help the poor, speak out against sin, and promote goodness, or we will suffer the effects of evil in our societies.

BIBLE EXTRA

Look up the following passages and summarize how Christians should behave in society.

Proverbs 21:5–8, 10–13

Proverbs 21:15–18, 21–28

2 Timothy 3:1–11

The disciplined person, one who knows strength of character and attitude built from real faith in and obedience to God, brings stability to relationships, especially family. Quarreling spouses and rebellious children destroy a society. Such bad behavior will result in a drunken, fearful, lazy, immoral society where people only wish to satisfy their selfish lusts. The healthy society, built on the disciplined ways of God, produces wise, responsible, happy people, the envy of all societies.

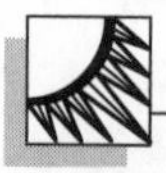

FAITH ALIVE

Christians can be involved in social affairs by voting, holding public office, participating in social service organizations, and other such activities. How do you involve yourself in community life?

How may God be at work in these areas, especially in non-Christian organizations and institutions?

1. W.O.E. Oesterley, *The Book of Proverbs* (London: Methuen and Co., Ltd., 1929), 155.

2. Ibid.

3. Samuel Fallows, *The Popular and Critical Bible Encyclopedia and Scriptural Dictionary*, (Chicago: Howard-Severance Co., 1916), 1:258.

Lesson 7/Thirty Thoughts of the Wise *(22:17—24:22)*

A Chinese Christian awoke one morning on his rice farm to find that the water was gone from his fields. The situation was mysterious because the farmer flooded his fields every night. One night, he crept stealthily to a prepared hiding place near his fields and watched his neighbor steal the water. The man broke out a portion of the earthen dike that kept the water in and let the water drain into his own fields. Then the neighbor carefully repaired the dike so that the break was hardly noticeable.

The Christian man prayed for an answer to this problem. His neighbor was not a Christian and was clearly stealing property not his own. Should the Christian report the man to the authorities? He had every legal right to do so. Should he confront his neighbor and demand repayment? Surely it was owed him, and maybe such a confrontation would stop the neighbor's theft in the future. But wouldn't confrontation anger the neighbor, though the Christian man was in the right? How could the grace of God be included in this problem?

As he prayed, the Christian man received a solution. That night, he flooded his fields as usual, but he also flooded his neighbor's fields. When he awoke the next morning, his fields, and his neighbor's, had water in them. He did the same thing for several nights. Finally one morning, he awoke to a pounding on his door. He opened it to see a very surprised neighbor who asked him why he had done such a thing. Clearly the neighbor knew that the Christian man was aware what had been happening to the water. Why should the Christian react in kindness and generosity, instead of anger and legal action?

The Christian man explained his faith in God and how God had shown him what to do as a result of his prayers. The neighbor had never seen or experienced such love, and immediately asked to become a Christian too.

Not only should we treat people as we wish to be treated (Matt. 7:12) but we should also treat people with love and kindness greater than what the situation usually calls for. Christians shouldn't react to others the way they might to us. We have the mind of Christ (1 Cor. 2:16) and the gift of the Holy Spirit (Acts 2:38) who sheds abroad, all around us, His love for all people (Rom. 5:5).

This next section of Proverbs is the first part of a group of wisdom sayings called "thoughts of the wise." The section contains thirty specific proverbs that instruct us in how to treat God, others, and ourselves properly for a successful, happy life.

Treat People Fairly (22:17—23:11)

The wise sages knew all kinds of people, and how to deal with them. They have specific reasons for giving us these thirty proverbs. Read the following passages from Proverbs and tell why the sages gave us each saying.

22:17, 18

22:19

22:20, 21

For the following passages, name the kinds of persons about whom the proverbs are written, and tell how we should deal with them.

22:22, 23

22:24, 25

22:26, 27

22:28; 23:10, 11

22:29

Though Proverbs 22 mentions several kinds of people whom we meet in our communities, Proverbs 23 names more of them. Name these people and tell how we should deal with them.

23:1–3

23:4, 5

23:6–8

23:9, 10

At Our Best

People do some great things. Nearly every day you can hear Paul Harvey or some other media personality relate a story or two about the heroics of a person who saw the need of another person and came to their rescue. People such as Mother Teresa or Larry Jones thrill our hearts with their sensitivity and compassion expressed through their humanitarian deeds of kindness. In fact, though we common folks do not get the same recognition, there are countless, similar deeds performed by average, everyday people on the behalf of their families, friends, and co-workers every day. Why? Because we know where others hurt, we have been there. We want to be the source of virtue, at least sometimes, in someone's life. We want to be helpful. It feels good. It feels right. We know it's the way we were meant to be.

Word Wealth

Twice in this section of Proverbs occurs the warning not to remove the ancient landmarks of property, yours or another person's (Prov. 22:28; 23:10). What does the law of Moses teach about anyone who moves a landmark? (Deut. 27:17)

What is one reason God gave such a strong command about respecting the property of others? (Josh. 13:1–7; Num. 33:53, 54)

What is another reason for God's warning not to move landmarks? (Ex. 20:15, 17; Lev. 19:11)

What things belong to God?
Leviticus 25:23

Leviticus 26:12

Leviticus 27:30

Treat Yourself Well (23:12—24:4)

Not only should we treat others fairly and generously, but there are certain things we should do for ourselves. Read the following passages from Proverbs and describe the things we should do to help ourselves live the abundant life.

23:12

23:15, 16, 19

23:17, 18; 24:1, 2

23:20, 21

23:27, 28

Why do we discipline children? (Prov. 23:13, 14)

When do we rejoice over our children? (Prov. 23:22–26)

WORD WEALTH

Proverbs 23:32 says that wine is like a serpent, a viper that bites and stings. Serpents in the Bible are usually poisonous snakes, like the viper, a mildly poisonous snake of some two feet long, red to brown with black markings, or the adder, larger and more deadly.[1]

The older English versions of the Bible sometimes translate serpent in Proverbs 23:32 as "cockatrice," which is a deadly snake.[2] The point of the verse is that wine can slip up on people, like a snake does, before they can recognize the danger, and "bite" harmfully.

The snake is used as a symbol of treachery, deceit, and hidden danger. Read the following passages and tell what role snakes play in the biblical situations.

Genesis 3:1–4

Numbers 21:4–9

John 3:14

Revelation 20:1–3

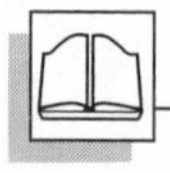

BIBLE EXTRA

The drunken man in Proverbs 23:34, 35 has climbed to the top of the mast of a ship, numbed by his wine, so that he experiences no pain. Obviously such behavior is foolishness.

Ships are mentioned many times in the Bible. Read the following passages and write out how the idea of a ship is used to teach us truth.

Isaiah 54:11

Job 9:26

Proverbs 31:14

I Timothy 1:19

Treat Life With Respect (24:5–22)

We must treat others fairly, and ourselves with wisdom. Now we consider how we treat life's problems and situations. Read the following Proverbs passages, name the problem situation, and tell what we are instructed to do about it.

24:5, 6

24:7–9

24:10

24:11

24:12, 21

Sometimes we encounter persecution or people who oppose us. Sometimes we are afflicted by the evil deeds of wicked people. What do these Proverbs instruct us to do to overcome these situations?

24:15, 16

24:17, 18

24:19, 20

24:21, 22

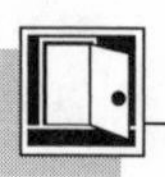

Behind the Scenes

Proverbs 24:20 says that "the lamp of the wicked will be put out." Lamps in ancient times were small oblong pots filled with olive oil, and a cloth wick, probably linen or flax, was inserted and lit. These lamps could be carried by hand or placed on shelves or lampstands built for such a purpose (Ex. 25:31–38).[3]

The picture in Proverbs 24:20 is that the lamp, a symbol for life, of the wicked will be put out, clearly a disastrous end. Read the following passages and write the other meanings for "lamp."

2 Samuel 22:29

Psalm 119:105

Proverbs 13:9

Daniel 10:6

Revelation 4:5

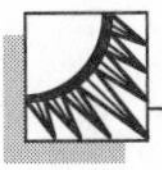

FAITH ALIVE

How does the Lord expect us to treat our enemies and those who hurt us?

Proverbs 24:17–20

Matthew 5:44

Luke 6:27, 35

Romans 5:10

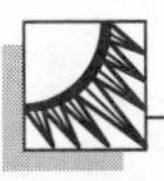

FAITH ALIVE

The Bible gives clear guidelines for the wise and careful use of the many gifts God has bestowed upon us. Listed below are just a few of the many passages that address the importance of being disciplined with regard to our time, material wealth, minds, and bodies.

Read each passage until you find a message that God has for your life at this time. Summarize that message in a few words in the space provided.

1. Time is short; use it well (Ps. 90:1–7; James 4:13–16).

2. Take time to be holy (Gen. 2:2–3; Ex. 20:8–11).

3. Redeem the time (Eph. 5:15–16; Matt. 20:1–16).

4. Tithing: managing material wealth (Gen. 14:17–24; 1 Chron. 29:11–16).

5. Good stewards of God's gifts (Hag. 1:2–6; 2:8).

6. Serving one another's need (Acts 4:32–35).

7. Our lifestyle and body (Rom. 12:1–2).

8. Our bodies belong to God (1 Tim. 4:12; 2 Tim. 2:22).

9. The temple of the Holy Ghost (1 Cor. 6:13–20).

10. Judgment on poor stewardship of the body (Rom. 1:18–32).

1. Robert S. Phillips (ed.), *Funk and Wagnalls New Encyclopedia* (New York: Funk and Wagnalls, Inc., 1975) 1:167, and *Merriam-Webster's Collegiate® Dictionary,* Tenth Edition © 1996 by Merriam Webster Inc.

2. Samuel Fallows, *The Popular and Critical Bible Encyclopedia and Scriptural Dictionary,* (Chicago: Howard-Severance Co., 1916), 1555, and *Merriam-Webster's Collegiate® Dictionary,* Tenth Ed.

3. Fallows, 1044, 1045.

Lesson 8/The Winning Ways of Wisdom (24:23–34)

The grasshopper played a merry tune on his fiddle as he watched the autumn sun rise to bring another bright and cheerful day. What a wonderful life is this, thought the grasshopper. He rejoiced in the brilliant colors of fall and danced a happy little dance.

"Best be storing up some food," remarked a busy little ant, who hurried by the grasshopper. The ant had his hands full, carrying grain to his hill.

"It'll be winter soon, and you won't feel like dancing then." The ant was always such a party spoiler.

"Oh, go on, ant! I've got plenty of time," crowed the grasshopper, as he danced a circle around his busy little friend.

"Well, don't say I didn't warn you," returned the ant. "And don't come crying to me when you get hungry!"

The grasshopper laughed scornfully and sang his way home, laughing at the memory of the ant—so busy, so glum, so miserable.

Winter did come soon, as the ant had said. The grasshopper hurried in panic to gather what remaining food he could find, but it was not enough. All his glee left him with the realization that the ant's advice, dull as it was at the time, was wise. His food ran out, and he starved.

This little story is based on Aesop's fable which highlights one idea, that the hard-working person rejoices after work is done, and the lazy person suffers when responsibilities are neglected. In the second part of the Thirty Thoughts of the Wise (Prov. 24:23–34), a similar contrast is made between the blessed and the poor, guiding us to the winning ways of wisdom.

BIBLE EXTRA

Proverbs 24:23 warns us that we must treat other people without favoritism. Read the following proverbs and answer the questions.

How does God view the ways we treat each other? (21:3)

What happens to the wicked who treat others badly? (21:7)

What do the righteous receive when they treat others properly? (21:15)

What does the New Testament teach about favoritism in the treatment of other people? (James 2:1–13)

HOW TO BECOME BLESSED (24:23–29)

The goals of our lives must include honoring God and blessing other people. Of course, we want to be blessed as well. In this section of Proverbs 24, we are shown some ways that we can become blessed in life. Read the passages and answer the questions.

How do the righteous treat others? (24:23)

How do the wicked twist the truth? (24:24)

How do the righteous receive a blessing? (24:25)

What kind of speaking will bless another person? (24:26)

How should righteous people do their work? (24:27)

Word Wealth

The idea of **blessing** in Proverbs is expressed in two Hebrew words, *barak* (*Strong's* #1288 & #1293) and *'asher* (*Strong's* #833 & #835). Together, they refer to the positive state of one who has received favor from, primarily, the Lord, as well as to specific acts of good will or gifts received from another, again, usually from the Lord. Blessing then includes the ideas of general prosperity and happiness, also the specific acts or gifts one receives or gives, and the human acts of pronouncing blessing upon God or others. Two notable occurences of *barak* are these:

> "The blessing of the Lord makes one rich,
> And He adds no sorrow with it." (Prov. 10:22)
>
> (The Lord to Abram)
> "I will bless you
> And make your name great;
> And you shall be a blessing.
> I will bless those who bless you,
> And I will curse him who curses you;
> And in you all the families of the earth shall be blessed." (Gen. 12:2–3)

Two occurrences of *'asher:*

> (Referring to the Messiah)
> "Men shall be blessed in Him;
> All nations shall call Him blessed." (Ps. 72:17)

(Of the virtuous woman)
"Her children rise up and call her blessed;
Her husband also, and he praises her." (Prov. 31:28)

While being blessed by God always has positive results, blessing does not always produce instant or superficial happiness. Job 5:17 speaks of a true blessing from God that few would describe as bringing instant happiness to them:

"Behold, happy is the man whom God corrects:
Therefore, do not despise the chastening of the Almighty."

BEHIND THE SCENES

Proverbs 24:26 says that "he who gives a right answer kisses the lips." Kissing the mouth, for the ancient Hebrews, primarily indicated affection or respect among close relatives or friends. This act also meant a great feeling of gratitude or joy as a result of someone's deeds.[1]

Read the following passages and describe the purpose or meaning of the kiss in each situation.

Genesis 29:13

Ruth 1:14

Proverbs 7:13

Mark 14:43–45

Luke 7:38

Acts 20:37

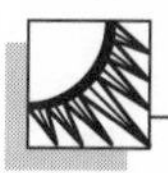

FAITH ALIVE

Because we are human, we will offend somebody sometime. And we will be wronged as well. Instead of taking revenge on the people who have treated us badly, how should we treat them?

Matthew 5:38–47

Romans 12:19–21

1 Corinthians 6:1–7

HOW TO BECOME POOR (24:30–34)

The ancient Hebrews realized that hard work produced good harvests. They also believed that lazy, irresponsible people will reap poverty and trouble. Read the following passages and answer the questions.

What does the lazy person lack? (Prov. 24:30)

What did the lazy person's field look like? (Prov. 24:31)

What did the author of the proverb gain by seeing the lazy person's field? (Prov. 24:32)

What lesson should we learn from the story of the lazy person? (Prov. 24:33–34)

Word Wealth

The author of the proverb describes the lazy person's field covered with thorns and nettles. Nettles are coarse plants "armed with stinging hairs,"[2] weeds with tiny, sharp hairs on their stems or leaves that produce an itching inflammation on the skin when touched.[3] Nettles are often connected with thorns and brambles (Is. 34:13) or other unpleasant plants and conditions (Zeph. 2:9).

Thorns, which include such unpleasant plants like nettles and thistles, are used in the Bible to convey various meanings. Read the following passages and write out the meaning of "thorns" in each one.

Proverbs 25:19

Proverbs 26:9

Hosea 2:6

Matthew 7:16

2 Corinthians 12:7

How to Become Rich

Clearly, the teaching of Proverbs describes prosperity as a blessing of God given to the hard-working, righteous person. Read the following proverbs and describe how prosperity comes.

3:16

22:4

24:4

28:13

Realistically, the ancient Hebrews knew other things about riches. Read the following proverbs and describe these other truths about riches.

11:4

11:28

13:7

23:5

27:24

Christian Busy-ness

We have all heard of the devout relative or friend who is at church "every time the door is open," as if only the truly dedicated are able to be there so much. They may only be dedicated to busy-ness. We have been working so hard to bring Christianity to the world that we have not noticed that we do not know, much less love, our neighbors; that we have lost touch with our children and spouses; that we have substituted programs for *spiritual* development and action for thought, understanding, and devotion.

The church is not a business to be run efficiently, but a haven for the troubled and for seekers of truth. The church is not a government that members must seek to rule, often at the expense and offense of other members, but a kingdom of priests, interceding to the King for the hurts and needs of fellow human beings.

Have we tried to re-create our national culture in the organization we call church? Are we in too much of a hurry, too programmed, too active to reflect, meditate, listen, see what is really around us, appreciate the miracles that happen every day or show love to people?

The peace at the core of true prosperity cannot be experienced by workaholism. Peaceful Christians emit peaceful "vibes"; people around them can perceive the residence of the Prince of Peace in their beings, in their lives. Peaceful Christians are content, not angry or frustrated, able to really *trust* God in all events of life. Joy is the external exhibition of the inner *well-being* and *hopefulness*, the demonstration of the truly happy life enjoyed by Christians who do not strive with life and God, but who rest in His provision.

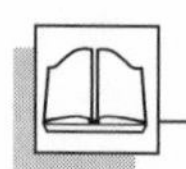

Bible Extra

Read the following passages, and describe what other parts of the Bible teach about prosperity and riches.

Malachi 3:10–12

Matthew 6:24–33; 13:22

2 Corinthians 9:6–11

Philippians 4:15–19

I Timothy 6:17

Clearly, God intends to bless His people, spiritually and financially, but we must guard our hearts that money does not become our god, the source in whom we trust. Notice that the righteous people in our lesson not only worked hard, but honored God by their attitudes and the way they treated other people. They reaped blessings from the blessings they sowed.

PROBING THE DEPTHS

Prosperity, Poverty, and Providence.

Every discussion about the righteous way to enjoy prosperity and to avoid poverty presupposes the doctrine of God's providence. Providence refers to the continuous activity of God in His creation by which He preserves and governs. The doctrine of providence affirms God's absolute lordship over His creation and confirms the dependence of all creation on the Creator. It is the denial of the idea that the universe is governed by chance or fate.

Through His providence God controls the universe (Ps. 103:19); the physical world (Matt. 5:45); the affairs of nations (Ps. 66:7); man's birth and destiny (Gal. 1:15); man's successes and failures (Luke 1:52); and the protection of His people (Ps. 4:8).

God preserves all things through His providence (1 Sam. 2:9; Acts 17:28). Without His continual care and activity the world would not exist, for it would be surrendered to the fallibility of mankind and the sinister devices of the devil (John 10:10). God also preserves His people through His providence (Gen. 28:15; Luke 21:18; 1 Cor. 10:13; 1 Pet. 3:12).

God's providence, then, is that divine government which sustains, the continued activity by which He directs all things to the ends He has chosen in His eternal plan. God is King of the universe who has given Christ all power and authority to reign (Matt. 28:18–20; Acts 2:36; Eph. 1:20–23). He governs even in insignificant things (Matt. 10:29–31), apparent accidents (Prov. 16:33), as well as man's good (Phil. 2:13) and evil deeds (Acts 14:16). This does not mean He *causes* all things, but that He is above and beyond all, and available to move into any situation and overthrow its destructive design. Regarding God's providential workings, two facts must be remembered:

1. God acts in accordance with the laws and principles that He has established in the world.

2. Man is free to choose and act independently from God's will and plan. While God is above man's choices and actions (Gen. 45:5; Deut. 8:18; Prov. 21:1), His actions never violate the reality of human choice or negate man's responsibility as a moral being. He may permit sinful acts to occur, but He does not cause man to sin nor is He responsible for sin's results (Gen. 45:5; Rom. 9:22). Still, in mercy, God's providence often overrules evil for good and transcends circumstances in bringing about His benevolent will (Gen. 50:20; Acts 3:13).[4]

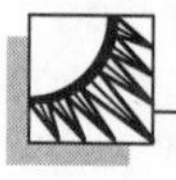

Faith Alive

Since we want to reap blessings in our lives, what blessings should we sow in other people's lives?

Matthew 5:12–15

Matthew 5:42–45

Matthew 7:12

1 John 4:7–11

What should we do toward God to receive His blessings?

Proverbs 3:7–10

Psalm 147:1, 11

Micah 6:8

James 1:27

1 John 2:3–6

1. Samuel Fallows, *The Popular and Critical Bible Encyclopedia and Scriptural Dictionary* (Chicago: Howard-Severance Co., 1916), 1032.

2. *Merriam-Webster's Collegiate® Dictionary*, Tenth Edition © 1996 by Merriam-Webster Inc.

3. Robert S. Phillips (ed.), *Funk and Wagnalls New Encyclopedia* (New York: Funk and Wagnalls, Inc., 1975), 17:255.

4. Jack Hayford (Gen. Ed.), *Hayford's Bible Handbook* (Nashville: Thomas Nelson, 1995), 737.

Lesson 9/Hezekiah's Handbook of Heroes
(25:1—29:27)

Kings and queens do not often have good moral and ethical reputations. In the recent movie *Braveheart*, the English king, Edward I, was cruel, heartless, and ruthless, about as bad as a king could get.

One king, however, was made a saint by the Roman church in 1297; he was Louis IX of France—St. Louis, for whom the city in Missouri is named. Louis was a model king, "the most chivalrous man of his age and the ideal medieval king."[1]

Louis IX was known for his just and righteous life. He reformed city governments in France so that governmental officials could not mistreat nor oppress common citizens. He built hospitals and developed programs for the care of lepers, the sick, the poor, and orphans. The Parliament of Paris and the first true nation of France were created by Louis' reforms. He was an arbiter of many European conflicts, a true peacemaker.

Above all, and the reason for his success, was Louis' religious devotion. He wore monk's robes and a hairshirt when he repented of sin; he confessed sins regularly and went to two Crusades to attempt the rescue of Jerusalem from enemy armies. His strong Christian morality led him to not only restrain such standard medieval practices as dueling, private wars of nobles, and jousting tournaments, but also to write a "courtesy book" (how-to instructional books like Proverbs which guided people through life) for his eleven children.[2]

Truly, Louis IX was an unusual king, one who took his faith in Christ seriously and practically. Such a lifestyle affected everything he did. He was a hero of the faith as well as a hero of his age.

The collection of Proverbs 25—29 consists of more sayings of Solomon collected by King Hezekiah's scribes, some 200 years after Solomon's reign. These proverbs describe heroic and not-so-heroic members of society, who teach us lessons to live by.

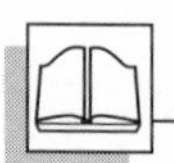

BIBLE EXTRA

The Bible says much to leaders, who are held responsible for how they lead other people.

Why did King Saul lose his kingdom? (1 Sam. 13:5–14; 15:6–23)

What should a king know about God's role in his kingdom? (Dan. 4:1–3; 5:18–23)

Why is Jehoshaphat a good example of a righteous king? (2 Chr. 17:1–6)

How did God come to Jehoshaphat's aid? (2 Chr. 20:1–24)

WISDOM FIT FOR A KING (25:1–28)

All societies have rulers and government. Proverbs tells us how best to rule and govern the people of God. Read the following passages and answer the questions.

If it is an honor for God to be mysterious, what is the honor for kings? (Prov. 25:2)

How can a ruler be successful? (Prov. 25:5)

How should we conduct ourselves before rulers? (Prov. 25:6, 7)

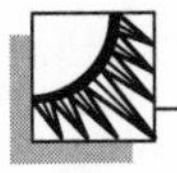

FAITH ALIVE

Our spiritual elders oversee our spiritual lives so that we may walk worthy of our calling in Christ. How does the Bible say we should act toward our spiritual elders?

1 Thessalonians 5:12, 13

1 Timothy 5:1, 2, 17–19

How does the Bible say we should act toward all those in authority over us?

1 Timothy 2:1–3

Titus 3:1, 2

WARNINGS ABOUT THE LAZY (26:1–28)

Whereas the righteous king is a real hero of faith, the lazy person is not a hero but an example *not* to follow. By warning us of all the bad things associated with the sluggard, Solomon can help us know what *to* do.

What picture does Solomon humorously use to illustrate the behavior of the lazy?
(Prov. 26:14)

How does Solomon use an exaggeration to show us the personality of the lazy? (Prov. 26:15)

Can a lazy person be taught? (Prov. 26:16)

WORD WEALTH

Proverbs 26 mentions another not-so-heroic figure, the fool. Interestingly, the Hebrew word for fool is represented in English as *evil*, which means a wrong-thinking person, whose conduct is not governed by common sense or righteousness. This kind of thinking results in unwise or bad actions, called "folly."[3] The Lord Jesus does not allow us to publicly call someone a fool because such a name implies that the person is utterly wicked and is going to hell (Matt. 5:22).[4]

Let's compare the wise person and the fool. Look up each verse, and list one or more characteristics of the wise and fools in the proper columns.

PROVERBS	WISE	FOOL
10:13		
15:14		
17:10		
18:6, 7		
18:15		
25:11–13		
26:7–11		

The Friend (27:1–27)

Who are your friends? Are they just people you like, or do they do things real friends do? Proverbs 27 illustrates what a real friend is.

What does Proverbs 27:5, 6 teach about frankness and honesty between friends?

What benefit is there in having friends? (Prov. 27:9)

What does Proverbs 27:14 teach about courtesy and kindness toward friends?

In the famous verse, Proverbs 27:17, what benefit do we receive from our friends?

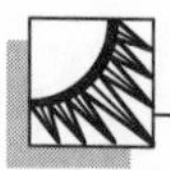

FAITH ALIVE

All of us like to be appreciated by others, but if we don't watch carefully, we can become conceited. What does Proverbs 27:1, 2 teach about boasting and receiving praise?

WARNINGS FOR THE RICH (28:1–28)

Most of us think we would like to win a lottery or "strike it rich." Since our society thrives on money, we can easily get caught up in the passion for it. Proverbs warns us that, though God's obedient people should expect to prosper, rich people who come to love their riches will have nothing but trouble.

When is it better to be poor than rich? (Prov. 28:6)

When does gaining riches become a useless activity? (Prov. 28:8)

What kind of people will prosper? (Prov. 28:13, 19, 27)

What happens to people who hurry to get rich? (Prov. 28:20, 22)

WORD WEALTH

Proverbs 28:8 teaches that business people who resort to usury to gain riches will ultimately lose all they have gained. Usury, in the Hebrew, is *nehshek*, which means "biting." The practice of usury is the loan of money which must be paid back with extra high interest. In the Law of Moses, loans could be made with reasonable interest to outsiders or non-Hebrews, but not to God's people (see Lev. 25:36, 37; Deut. 23:19, 20).[5]

What does Ezekiel 18:8, 13 teach about how people misused usury?

What did Nehemiah do to deal with usury? (Neh. 5:10, 11)

What does the New Testament teach about usury?
Matthew 25:27

Luke 6:30, 35

Luke 19:23

Wisdom for the Righteous (29:1–27)

The real heroes are the righteous. Over eighty sayings in Proverbs describe the righteous people as the blessed of God, who bless the world with their lives.

What does Proverbs 29:2, 4, 14 teach about righteous people in authority?

Why are righteous people happy? (Prov. 29:6, 16, 18, 25)

How do righteous people treat other people? (Prov. 29:7, 10, 27)

Word Wealth

In Proverbs 29:27, we learn that to righteous people, wickedness is an abomination. Several Hebrew words are translated "abomination," which means filth, uncleanness, rejection, disgust, impurity, or pollution. The basic idea of abomination certainly is that particular practices that people do are so vile that they must be rejected and abandoned by God's people.

What things were abominations to the Egyptians? (Gen. 43:32; 46:34; Ex. 8:25, 26)

What things were abominations to Hebrews? (John 18:28; Acts 10:28; 11:13)[6]

What things are abominations to Christians? (Lev. 18:6, 21–25; Deut. 27:15–26; Luke 16:14,15)

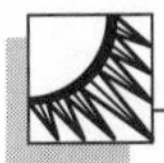

FAITH ALIVE

According to these proverbs, how should we treat our friends?

17:17

18:24

27:6

What are ways *not* to treat friends?

17:9

27:10

What does Proverbs teach about false friends? (Prov. 19:6)

1. William L. Langer (ed.), *An Encyclopedia of World History* (Boston: Houghton Mifflin Co., 1948, 5th ed. © 1972), 230. Reprinted by permission of Houghton Mifflin Company. All rights reserved.

2. Joseph R. Strayer (ed.), *Dictionary of the Middle Ages* (New York: Charles Scribner's Sons, 1987), 3:366, 7:675–676, Langer, 230.

3. Samuel Fallows, *The Popular and Critical Bible Encyclopedia and Scriptural Dictionary*, (Chicago: Howard-Severance Co., 1916), 669.

4. Fallows, 667.

5. Fallows, 1693, 1694.

6. Fallows, 21, 22.

Lesson 10/Agur's Axioms (30:1–33)

Edgar always had a deal in the works. "Just one more," he'd say, "then we'll be on easy street." But the "one more" never panned out. Edgar hopped from one job to another; first he was a shoe salesman, then a restaurant owner, a wheat farmer, an insurance salesman, and finally a video arcade manager. He never seemed content and happy with his current job; there was always something better at the end of the rainbow.

Some of us are that way with our church memberships or other relationships. As soon as we find something *not* perfect, we're off to find something or someone else. Edgar never reached his pot of gold at the end of the rainbow. A tireless quest for "change" won't satisfy us either. Only Jesus Himself will satisfy us and in Him we rest contentedly.

We are helpless and lost without God, who keeps all His promises. Our best state of life is contentment, being neither rich nor poor. Such a life is free from the temptations to disobey God by stealing or cheating to relieve the stress of our needs and to neglect God because our wealth removes our feelings of need for Him.

WORD WEALTH

Utterance, used in Proverbs 30:1 is also translated "prophecy" in many of the prophetic books of the Old Testament (see Is. 21:1; Hos. 1:1). The term generally refers to a word God speaks, given through direct personal revelation (Jer. 1:2), dreams and visions (Dan. 7:1),[1] or visitations by God or His representatives (Matt. 1:20, 21; 3:17; Luke 1:13–20, 28–37). In the case of Proverbs 30, the term probably means a message inspired by God or serious, godly words that must be heeded.

Some things in life are never satisfied; some cannot be explained; some are intolerable but some are clever. Some things are impressive in their appearance, performance, or being; but all these qualities are gifts of God, whether people recognize Him or not. God made life exciting, unusual, and interesting; we respond to His world as we do to Him, with awe, respect, and wonder.

Neither Rich nor Poor (30:1–14)

The unknown author of Proverbs 30, Agur the son of Jakeh, expresses first his utter helplessness as a man and how much he needs God. "I have wearied myself," he repeats, as he criticizes his own lack of wisdom and knowledge of God. Sometimes, when we think about the mysteries in life, the unusual happenings and how God is involved, and just who God really is, we realize how humble and weak we are. This is what Agur has done.

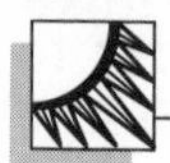

Faith Alive

List the questions Agur asks in Proverbs 30:4 and describe how each characterizes God.

How do these questions make you feel?

Now read 30:5 and describe the reassurance given by that verse.

Agur is awed by God and life, but how does he put things in proper perspective?

Who must be first in our lives ? (Prov. 30:4, 5)

Why are we dependent upon God? (Prov. 30:2, 3)

What does God do for us? (Prov. 30:5)

Agur is also concerned that he not depart from his faith in God, and so he prays a unique prayer. What two things does he ask for?

30:7, 8

30:8, 9

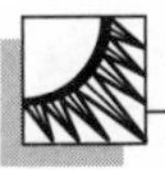

FAITH ALIVE

Was Agur's prayer good or bad?

Why?

How would you share with him to answer his concerns?

Agur's last concern was for the younger generation of his day (30:11–14). You see, ours is not the only time when older people despaired of the future of the generations.

What bad thing did Agur hear young people say about their parents? (Prov. 30:11)

What attitude did the young people have about themselves? (Prov. 30:12, 13)

What other shameless acts did the young people do? (Prov. 30:14)

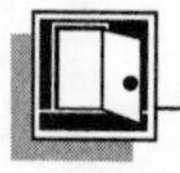

BEHIND THE SCENES

Adolescence, or teenagers as a class of people with unique social problems, is a modern creation of Western culture. In Bible times, a young man was apprenticed to a craftsman, scholar, or some other occupation soon after his twelfth birthday. He was expected to work for his own living within just a few years. Young women were taught domestic skills in the home and married by the time they were 14 or 15 years old to start a family of their own. Obviously this circumstance did not keep some irresponsible youths from neglecting these social customs.

THE UNSATISFIED FOUR (30:15–17)

Agur cleverly arranges the next series of wise sayings in groups of four, which makes them easier to understand and remember. The first group of four are unsatisfied, "bottomless pits" that can never get enough.

Name these four and tell why they cannot be filled (Prov. 30:16).

1.

2.

3.

4.

WORD WEALTH

The leech of Proverbs 30:15 cries out, "Give, give!" The Hebrew phrase here is symbolic and refers to a legendary flesh-eating ghost or demon who supposedly had two daughters named for two terrible diseases.[2] This demon later became associated with Gehenna, the Valley of Hinnon—a picture of the lake of fire and eternal judgment (Rev. 20:14; Matt. 5:22, 29).

The animal used as a representative of this evil legend is the horseleech, a blood-sucking leech found in stagnant water, a representation of a vampire or blood-sucking "night monster."[3]

WORD WEALTH

Sheol (pronounced shay-*ole*), is the Hebrew word for world of the dead, a place where departed spirits went, many believe, until the resurrection of Jesus. The place was considered invisible, where each person would meet departed loved ones (see Gen. 25:8; 35:29).[4] This concept is different from hell, which is the eternal place of punishment for evil. The corresponding Greek word is ***hades*** (*hā*dees). W. E. Vine says "It never denotes the grave, nor is it the permanent region of the lost; . . . it is, for such, intermediate between decease and the doom of Gehenna," or hell.[5]

BIBLE EXTRA

Look up the following passages and summarize the biblical teaching about *sheol* and *hades*:

2 Samuel 22:6

Job 11:8

Psalm 16:10

Psalm 139:8

Luke 16:19–31

BIBLE EXTRA

Proverbs 30:17 refers to a child who mocks and disobeys parents. One way the Hebrew is translated suggests that such a person ought to be dragged out into the wilderness to be eaten by scavengers. Such a statement clearly displays the disgust felt about such behavior.

What punishment was required for children who cursed parents? (Lev. 20:9)

What happens if sin and disrespect are allowed to go unpunished? (Josh. 7:1, 13, 15)

Look up the following passages and tell what Christ has done to deliver us from curses and evil behavior.

Galatians 3:10–13

Revelation 22:3

2 Corinthians 5:21

I Peter 2:24

The Mysterious Four (30:18–20)

The next group of four astound Agur; he cannot understand them; they are mysterious. Name each one and explain why they are mysterious.

1.

2.

3.

4.

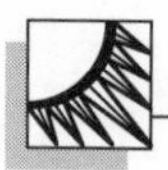

Faith Alive

The bumblebee shouldn't be able to fly. Its body is much too large in proportion to the size and number of its wings. But it doesn't know that and just flies anyway—the way God made it. How would our Christian lives be different if we simply believed God and took His Word for just what it says? In what areas does God challenge you to believe Him more fully?

The Intolerable Four (30:21–23)

The third group of four describes certain people who are intolerable, odious to society because of their characters.

Name each of these people and explain why they are intolerable.

1.

2.

3.

4.

WORD WEALTH

Every word of God is *pure*, meaning that the words are "refined," precise as possible, clear and useful for the purpose to which they are sent. God's words are not careless; they have meaning, purpose, and power. Modern people tend to think of words as simply noise, but what does the Bible teach about the power of words?

Genesis 1:1

Luke 4:36

Acts 3:6; Philippians 2:9–10

1 Corinthians 12:7–10

THE CLEVER FOUR (30:24–28)

The fourth group of four are the clever ones, who live "by their wits," not by their might.

Name each one and tell why they are clever.

1.

2.

3.

4.

The Impressive Four (30:29–31)

Finally, the fifth group of four are impressive in appearance. They each have something about them that stands out as we observe their comings and goings.

Name each one and tell why each is impressive.

1.

2.

3.

4.

BEHIND THE SCENES

The verbs in Proverbs 30:33, churning of milk, wringing of the nose, and forcing of wrath are all the same one, which means "pressing."[6] This use of words is humorous and draws a picture for us.

How are these three actions similar?

The Hebrew word "butter" is also used in a figurative sense to mean *great prosperity* (Job 29:6, to "wash one's steps with butter," probably melted butter of oily consistency) and *flattering speech* (Ps. 55:21, speech "smoother than butter," soft and agreeable).[7]

From these five groups of significant things what do we learn about

(a) the creativity of God?

(b) the nature and character of God?

(c) the wisdom of God?

Contentment with life is a great blessing (1 Tim. 6:6) from the Lord, who has made us and our world in such ways as to enliven and enrich life. If we are so narrow-minded that we seek only perishable riches or temporarily full stomachs, we suffer great emptiness. We miss God's grandeur and fail to trust Him when we live life selfishly and refuse to acknowledge His mystery and holiness. We can be clever in good ways and impressive in our accomplishments, but ultimately all honor and glory are His.

1. Samuel Fallows, *The Popular and Critical Bible Encyclopedia and Scriptural Dictionary* (Chicago: Howard-Severance Co., 1916), 1264.

2. Fallows, 829.

3. W.O.E. Oesterley, *The Book of Proverbs* (London: Methuen and Co., Ltd., 1929), 275.

4. Fallows, 1572–1573, Vol. III.

5. W. E. Vine, *et al, Vine's Complete Expository Dictionary of Old and New Testament Words* (Nashville: Thomas Nelson, 1984), 286.

6. Oesterley, 280.

7. Fallows, 317.

Lesson 11/Mom's Maxims
(31:1–9)

"Oh, Mom!" Billy stomped out of the kitchen through the back door.

"Billy, remember to talk to your teacher about your homework," his mother called after him. "You can't lose anything by asking."

"Alright, alright," replied Billy angrily. Mom was always giving advice: Do this, do that. He was sick of it.

"Hiya, sport!" it was Andy, Billy's best friend, who came up the alley to meet him. "You look really bent outta shape today, Billy Boy."

"Yeah," answered Billy, with a sad tone. "Mom's at it again. She oughta be in the papers, like Ann Landers or somebody."

"Sure, I know what you mean," said Andy.

"You mean your mom does that, too?" asked Billy. He thought he was the Lone Ranger when it came to mothers' nagging.

"Oh, sure. Everybody's mom does that," answered Andy. "All moms just seem to be that way, I think."

"Why?"

"You know, I'm sure they mean well," said Andy. "'Cause a lot of the things they say are helpful. At least they have been to me . . . when I listen."

"You listen to that stuff?"

"Well, most of the time . . . now."

"How come?"

"One day last year I did what my mom told me to," said Andy. "I had to apologize to Coach Beard for what I had said about him to the guys. And, well, it turned out just like Mom said it would, and me and Coach are best buddies now! So I figured maybe I should try some of the other stuff she says."

"And it really works, huh?" asked Billy.

"Yep, nearly every time."

"Not *every* time?"

"Well, nobody's perfect!"

In Proverbs 31, King Lemuel's mother left him good advice for leaders. Inordinate affection or lust for sex has destroyed many rulers, leaders, and their careers. Alcohol and the "party life" has also contributed to the destruction of too many lives. It is best for rulers and leaders to avoid these things completely and to help people in need—the helpless and oppressed, the poor and the weak.

Word Wealth

Chapter 31 of Proverbs opens with a reference to King Lemuel. This ruler has left no other record of his reign, no location or time in history. Some scholars believe his name is a veiled reference to Solomon, whose mother was Bathsheba. Probably Lemuel was a real king, not Solomon, but his history is unknown because the lessons his mother teaches are applicable to *all* rulers, at *any* time in history.[1]

Watch the Women (31:1–3)

Lemuel's mother is unnamed, but she had very definite ideas and concerns about her son's reign. She taught him these truths (see Prov. 1:8) that he might be a successful and beloved ruler.

What was her first concern, the problem that caused the greatest Hebrew king, Solomon, to turn from God and ruin his kingdom? (Prov. 31:3)

What was her advice to her son?

Solomon gathered foreign (non-Hebrew) women from pagan countries, 700 as wives and another 300 as concubines. Although many of these relationships were entered into to form political alliances, these women turned his heart away from the worship of God and obedience to His principles even to the point of Solomon's actually participating in the worship of idols, the gods of his women. As a result, Solomon's kingdom was destroyed, split in two, and brought incalculable death and destruction to the people of God (1 Kin. 11:1–13).

In modern society, we have seen both men and women ruin careers by unwise marital choices and immoral sexual behavior. Such acts break whatever fellowship a person has with God as well as ruin human relationships.

According to these passages in Proverbs, what results occur when we ignore the advice of Lemuel's mom?

2:16–19

5:3–23

7:5–27

9:13–18

WORD WEALTH

Chastisement refers to an infliction of punishment (as by whipping or beating). In the Bible the term chastisement usually refers to corrective punishment or discipline inflicted by God for the purpose of (1) education, instruction, and training (Job 4:3; Ps. 6:7); (2) corrective guidance (2 Tim. 2:25);

and (3) discipline, in the sense of corrective physical punishment (Prov. 22:15; Heb. 12:5–11; Rev. 3:19).

The most dramatic use of this word in the Bible is in Isaiah 53, in Isaiah's portrait of the Suffering Servant: "He was wounded for our transgressions, He was bruised for our iniquities; the chastisement for our peace was upon Him, and by His stripes we are healed" (Is. 53:5).

The New Testament reveals that Isaiah was speaking of Jesus Christ, who (a) died in our place, and for our sins, and who (b) bore the pain of our sicknesses in our behalf as well as the punishment for our sinning (Matt. 8:16–17; 1 Pet. 2:24).

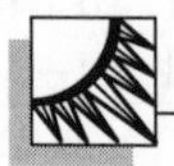

FAITH ALIVE

What safeguards should we employ to keep our lives morally pure? (Prov. 3:1–15)

How does the Holy Spirit help us? (1 Cor. 10:13 and Eph. 6:10–18)

BEHIND THE SCENES

The Old Testament distinguishes between adultery and fornication based on the marital status of the woman. Its concept of adultery involved a married or engaged woman having sexual relations with any man not her husband. Thus both the married woman and the man (married or single) were adulterers.

What penalties for this behavior were required? (Deut. 22:22–30; Lev. 19:20; 20:10–14)

Sex between a man and an unmarried woman was classified as fornication. Because the woman was unmarried, she had no spouse or legitimate children to be harmed. Fornication was still a great sin, more of a personal wrong; but adultery was personal *and* social, with negative effects on the whole community.[2]

What penalties for fornication were commanded?

Leviticus 20:17–21

Deuteronomy 22:28, 29

Exodus 22:16, 17

This way of defining adultery has broadened in contemporary times to include any sexual relationship with a person not one's husband or wife. As *Nelson's New Illustrated Bible Dictionary* notes, "The technical distinction between fornication and adultery is that adultery involves married persons, while fornication involves at least one person who is unmarried." Yet, "Jesus expanded the meaning of adultery to include the cultivation of lust: 'Whoever looks at a woman to lust for her has already committed adultery with her in his heart' (Matt. 5:28)."[3]

All forms of unchastity rob those who participate in them from God's ideal and created order for a man and woman to be joined as one in the faithful, loving, and permanent bond of marriage. Fornication and adultery always steal from personal, family, and national well being. The wisdom of Proverbs in this area is as valuable today as it has ever been for men and women.

Avoid the Alcohol (31:4–7)

Lemuel's mother knew that kings must be ever alert, vigilant rulers who knew and practiced the law rightly. Justice is a strong indicator of good government. Sadly, some people suffer injustice from their judicial system and governmental agencies.

What was the second concern of Lemuel's mother? (Prov. 31:4, 5)

What advice did she give him? (Prov. 31:6, 7)

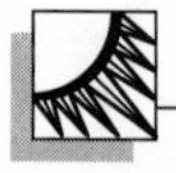

Faith Alive

In America, the drunkenness of a Christian is clearly a bad witness. Why do even many non-believing Americans consider any drinking to be unwise?

What other kinds of behavior, because of our witness as ambassadors of Christ, must we avoid? (1 Cor. 8:1–13; 9:11–15).

Word Wealth

King (*melek* in Hebrew) not only indicates the power to rule, such as our leaders in democratic countries enjoy, but carries a further meaning of "sure rule" or the last and final word, an absolute rule with which no one else can compete. The king should maintain the law, especially the laws of God, or he will destroy his kingdom; but the idea of revolution and rule by the will of the people is not even considered. Jesus is King of all kings, Ruler over all rulers, the absolute Monarch of all Creation (1 Tim. 1:17; 6:15). Sometimes we get used to a casual worship of God and forget His majesty, power, and privileges (see Luke 12:4–10; Matt. 7:21–23).[4]

BIBLE EXTRA

Several Hebrew words are translated "strong drink" or wine: *Tiyrosh* (Gen. 27:28) means new sweet wine, fresh, and not very fermented, but *Yayin* (Gen. 9:21; 49:12) means fermented wine, banquet wine. Clearly, Lemuel's mother wished her son to avoid the more intoxicating beverages, so his reason and discernment would remain clear. The strong stuff was reserved for sick and dying persons. In the New Testament all references to wine refer to *yayin*, basic dinner wine, except the passage in Acts 2:13, where the word is *gleukos* in Greek. This word means a sweet, highly intoxicating wine, fresh and newly made.[5]

PROTECT THE POWERLESS (31:8, 9)

Finally, Lemuel's mother addresses the positive, what kings *should* do.

What advice does she give her son? (Prov. 31:8, 9)

Lemuel must also judge rightly, and not be fooled or influenced by the wealthy or politically powerful, and he must help the poor and needy.

What does the Bible teach about judging rightly? (James 2:1–13)

1 John 4:1–3

1 Corinthians 6:1–8

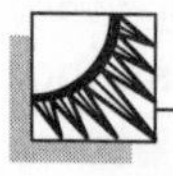

FAITH ALIVE

What can the church do today to speak for those who cannot speak for themselves? (James 1:27; Heb. 12:12–15)

How should we help those who are oppressed and suffering in our society? (Matt. 5:43–47; Luke 10:30–37)

1. Samuel Fallows, *Popular and Critical Encyclopedia and Scriptural Dictionary* (Chicago: Howard-Severance Co., 1916), Vol. II, 1056.

2. Fallows, Vol. I, 60–61.

3. Ronald F. Youngblood, Gen. Ed., "Adultery," "Fornication," *Nelson's New Illustrated Bible Dictionary*, (Nashville: Thomas Nelson, 1995).

4. James Strong, *New Strong's™ Exhaustive Concordance* (Nashville: Thomas Nelson, 1984), "Dictionary of the Hebrew Bible" #67.

5. Strong, #283, #284, #982, #983, #1174, #49, #67, #81, #90, #116, #124, "Dictionary of the Greek Testament" *#20, #51*.

Lesson 12/The Worthy Woman
(31:10–31)

She is someone who is admired. What can I say? She does so much for so many people. I can't keep track of it all.

People are drawn to her; they confide their deepest, most personal troubles to her and she calms and encourages them. She won't turn away anyone in need.

She walks for exercise around the local high school track every morning. Lots of people in town do too. She became friends with an eighty-year-old man, a widower who developed lung cancer. She encouraged him, listening to his tales of nostalgia as they walked around the track. She brought him to an assurance of his salvation before he died last fall.

She organizes the city-wide book sale at the library; book donations, volunteer workers, work schedules, business support, newspaper coverage, a really big event. It always turns out well. In spite of these and other activities, she loves us, her family; washes our clothes, keeps our busy calendar (husband and four children), and gives us all the personal attention we need.

Above all, she is a spiritual woman who loves Jesus and walks what she talks. I can testify to all this ability. I know her well; her name is Chrissy. I'm her husband.

Like my wife, a worthy woman is capable; she works hard and well at what she does, takes care of her family responsibilities, and discerns the good and bad of social and relational situations. A worthy woman is concerned about her loved ones and provides for them; she is also concerned about the poor and the affairs of her community, so that she takes action to help. A worthy woman is a great blessing to all those around her.

FAITH ALIVE

Consider how Jesus has made us all worthy in the sight of God. Read the following passages and summarize the biblical teaching about worthiness.

Matthew 10:37, 38

Acts 5:41

Ephesians 4:1–3

Hebrews 3:3

Revelation 4:11

THE CAPABLE WOMAN (31:10–19)

"Who can find a virtuous wife?" asked the author of Proverbs (31:10), for such a person is extremely valuable. In this passage, "virtuous" does not mean moral character; that issue is considered in 31:25, 26, and 30. Here the word means valiant, strong, more of a great force, and resourceful.[1] So, who can find a wife of resourcefulness, a great force in life? Such a person is worth more than rubies.

BIBLE EXTRA

Rubies are red sapphire stones that have been valuable in almost every culture in history. In the case of Proverbs 31, the stone is probably the oriental ruby, known for its bright red color and valued second only to diamonds.[2]

This Hebrew word, translated "ruby," occurs only six times in the Old Testament, and not at all in the New Testament. The Old Testament word is used only in poetry.

What does Job say compares to rubies? (Job 28:18)

Why does Jeremiah weep when he thinks of rubies? (Lam. 4:7)

The other four places where the word occurs are in Proverbs. What three things does Proverbs compare to the value of rubies?

1. 3:15

2. 20:15

3. 31:18

Why is this woman so valuable? (Prov. 31:11)

What are the results of her trustworthiness? (Prov. 31:12)

This woman is capable. What things does she do?
31:13

31:14

31:15

31:16

31:19

No wonder she is valued; she is talented, hard-working, resourceful, and shrewd. In other words, she works as hard as she can with all her abilities. Any person who does that will be valuable.

Behind the Scenes

In Proverbs 31:14 and 15, the worthy woman provides food for her family. Bread was the main staple of the diet, made from barley, wheat, or spelt. The grains were crushed and made into flour, usually by rubbing the grains between a small stone and a large one. The flour was mixed with olive oil or water and then kneaded with a reserve of yeast. Each day some leavened dough was kept in reserve for the next day's baking. The dough was then flattened into round shapes and baked usually in a clay oven, heated by coals from wood.

People also ate grapes, raisins, figs (fresh and dried), dates, and olives. The dates were used to make a special sweet sauce for Passover; and olives produced oil and were used for cooking, lamps, medicine, and personal hygiene. Almonds and other nuts, as well as citrus fruits, were also eaten. Beans, leeks, onions, cucumbers, melons, lentils, and peas were common vegetables. Milk from goats was made into cheese, and some people kept hens for eggs.

Lamb and beef were common meats eaten, as well as fish and some wild game. Salt was a valuable resource for flavor and preserving food. Bread was used often as a utensil for dipping into food and taking into the mouth.[3]

A Woman Concerned for Others (31:20–27)

Not only is the virtuous woman capable, but she is also concerned for the unfortunate of her community, for her family's protection from the elements of climate, for sufficient income to keep up the family and community, and for herself.

How does this good woman help her community?

31:20

31:26

31:27

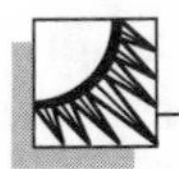

Faith Alive

Based on the example of this woman, in what ways can the church reach out to the poor and needy of our communities?

How can we reach out to other cultures, foreigners, and the social outcasts with the gospel of Christ?

WORD WEALTH

The word "scarlet" in Proverbs 31:21 refers to a costly, heavy red outer garment or robe which would easily keep a person warm in Middle Eastern winters, even with snow. The Greek and Latin versions of the Old Testament translate the Hebrew word as "double," which indicates the heavy nature of the cloth. Such garments were not worn by lower class people or servants, again revealing that the author of Proverbs does not consider being "well-to-do" an expectation unworthy of people blessed of God.[4]

For herself, the worthy woman makes clothing of fine linen and purple, again not a common material.

What does she do to decorate her home? (Prov. 31:22).

Her husband is a respectable, recognized citizen who interacts with other important people in the city gates. The "gates" of the cities were large open areas where markets were set up and political issues were discussed. Business deals were arranged in these areas as well as some marriages (Ruth 4:1–12).

This resourceful woman also made and sold linen garments, as well as supplied merchants with sashes, or garments worn around the waist and torso.

What clothes this woman besides garments? (Prov. 31:25)

WORD WEALTH

Linen garments (Prov. 31:24) were probably night gowns, thin sheets of costly linen to wrap the body. These garments could also be undergarments, linen wrappers, or could be used as outer garments over other attire. Sashes (31:24) are probably girdles, attire for the mid-section.[5]

For herself, the worthy woman is concerned, not for attire or physical objects, but that she speaks with wisdom and kindness, even when circumstances are difficult.

How does she become involved with business affairs?

31:26, 27

31:14–16

31:24

BIBLE EXTRA

Women have always been powerful and important in the Bible. Though the legal and inheritance systems favored men, women played responsible and important roles in society as well as in the church.

How have women been involved in critical events of Bible history?

Judges 4:4—5:31

Exodus 15:20

Esther 7:3, 4

Matthew 1:5, 17

The list of important women includes Eve, Sarah, Rebecca, Rachel, Hagar, Zipporah, Jael, Bathsheba, and others in the Old Testament.

In the New Testament, the Lord honors women with attention to their faith and leadership.

Whom did God inspire to prophesy about John the Baptist and Jesus? (Luke 1:41–55)

Many women followed the ministry of Jesus, even those with money and position (Luke 8:3). Women disciples were there in Jerusalem (Acts 1:14) and were filled with the Spirit at Pentecost (Acts 2:3).

Name some women who were involved in ministry in the early church.

Acts 16:14–15

Acts 9:36

1 Corinthians 1:11

Acts 18:2

These women played significant roles in the spread of the Gospel. This list also includes Candace, Queen of Ethiopia (Acts 8:27), Lois (2 Tim. 1:5), Eunice (2 Tim. 1:5), and others (2 Tim. 4:21).

How many women does Paul name in Romans 16 who were vital parts of his life and ministry?

The point is that the Lord has always valued and honored the work and character of women. Though Proverbs contrasted bad and good women, you will notice there are more passages that identify and contrast the various types of good and bad men. Women have always made significant and critically important contributions to the work and plan of God in history with His people and the spread of the gospel.

A Woman to be Commended (31:28–31)

Not only is the worthy woman capable and concerned but, because of her responsible attitude and productive activity, she is also commended.

How does Proverbs say she is honored? (Prov. 31:28, 29)

What is the highest praise she receives? (Prov. 31:30, 31)

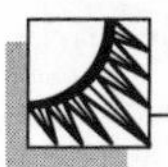

Faith Alive

Name some ways we can individually demonstrate godly character in our daily lives.

How has God developed godliness in your character?

Word Wealth

The word "charm" or "favor" in Proverbs 31:30 means "grace, comeliness," a physical attractiveness or gracefulness based on physical beauty. Such attributes are called "deceitful, vain," which means in Hebrew a "vapor or breath"; clearly the idea means "quickly passing," qualities that are here today and gone tomorrow. Any person who depends on physical beauty to gain praise and honor will eventually lose it all when the physical comeliness disappears. Only the spiritually beautiful and godly person will carry true respectability and honor from people and God.[6]

BIBLE EXTRA

The portrait of the virtuous wife closes with the key to her success (v. 30). Illustrating the theme of wisdom found throughout Proverbs, this woman first feared and reverenced God. Therefore, relationships and responsibilities were wisely balanced. She exemplifies the truth spoken by Jesus Christ, "Seek first the kingdom of God and His righteousness, and all these things shall be added to you" (Matt. 6:33). A close look at this woman can prove invaluable in helping every woman set her own priorities in managing the tme, resources, and giftedness God has given.[7]

Some scholars believe that the Proverbs 31 description of the worthy woman is too much for any one individual person and, therefore, must be a symbol or example of Lady Wisdom, in Proverbs 8 and 9. However, the tasks and character described in Proverbs 31 do not require that every woman do all these things, but merely provide general principles for men and women to live by. Industry, economic wisdom, provision of family needs, and management of business are some of the external evidences of the strong inner character that makes people dear to their families and communities. This woman wisely uses her resources for noble and proper ends; she speaks wisdom, does good to her loved ones, and honors the Lord in all things. Certainly any person would desire such a reputation.

BIBLE EXTRA

Being a godly wife begins with the right priorities—nourishing her personal relationship to God (Matt. 6:33), ministering to her husband (Prov. 18:22; 19:14), nurturing her children (2 Tim. 1:5), keeping her home (Titus 2:5), then adding whatever other activities time and energy permit. (Prov. 31:10–31).

A wife also has unique needs that are best met by her own husband:

- Spiritual leadership, including family worship of prayer and Bible study (1 Pet. 3:7)
- Personal affirmation (Eph. 5:25)
- Tender loving care, including touching, courtesies, and loving words (Prov. 5:19)
- Intimate, sensitive, and understanding communication (Song 2:16)
- Integrity worthy of respect and transparency so that nothing is hidden (Gen. 2:25)
- Provision and sustenance as well as protection (Gen. 2:15)
- Commitment of loyal devotion (Eccl. 9:9)

Scripture describes the creation of woman with the word "made" (Heb. *banah,* lit. "build"). God planned and supervised this "building" of the woman with the intent that she would be a "helper comparable to the man" (Heb. *'ezer kenegdo*). Unlike the animals, the woman was of the same nature as the man (Gen. 2:23). The word "helper" is also used to describe God (Ps. 33:20). It is a term of function rather than worth. A woman does not lose value as a person by humbly assuming the role of a helper.

The wife then has the assignment of being her husband's helper: (1) as a spiritual partner, assisting him in obeying the Word of God and in doing spiritual ministries, (2) as a counterpart in linking hands with the Creator to continue the generations, (3) as a confidant to offer comfort and fellowship (Gen. 2:23, 24), and (4) as a companion to provide encouragement and inspiration.[8]

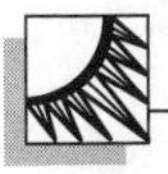

FAITH ALIVE

We must value each other for what God has put in us and called us to do.

How are we to relate to each other in Christ? (1 Cor. 12:12–27)

Since we did not choose our parents, our race, our culture, we must know that God has ordained all these for us, to make us who we are. And we should be satisfied with them; they are God's investments in us.

How do we make use of His gifts to glorify Him? (Matt. 5:16)

1. James Strong, *New Strong's™ Exhaustive Concordance* (Nashville: Thomas Nelson, 1984), "Dictionary to the Hebrew Bible," #1099, #39.

2. Samuel Fallows, *The Popular and Critical Bible Encyclopedia and Scriptural Dictionary* (Chicago: Howard-Severance Co., 1916), 1494.

3. Pat Alexander (ed.), *Eerdmans' Family Encyclopedia of the Bible* (Carmel, NY: Guideposts, 1978), 217–219.

4. W.O.E. Oesterley, *The Book of Proverbs* (London: Methuen and Co., Ltd., 1929), 285.

5. Oesterley, 286.

6. Oesterley, 287.

7. *The Woman's Study Bible,* Dorothy Patterson, Gen. Ed. (Nashville: Thomas Nelson, 1995), 1080.

8. Ibid., 1081.

Epilogue

Congratulations on completing your study of the Book of Proverbs! I hope you will now apply knowledge from this study to the living of a truly good and God-centered life. That is what the wisdom of Proverbs is all about.

It's time for you to take stock of the dimensions of wisdom you need the most now. Review the chart in Lesson 1, page 18, where you listed situations in your life for which you wanted God's wisdom. Complete that chart, taking time to review each lesson, so you will survey Proverbs again.

Once you've completed that chart, take time to pray, asking God to impress upon you one piece of advice, warning, or description you need to apply in your life as a top priority.

After you have prayed, write the items requested below:

1. Write the advice, warning, or description here:

2. Review Proverbs and list all the references you find that relate directly to what you wrote for 1.

3. Look up, read, and think about all these passages in Proverbs.

4. Now write a brief summary of the key point for your life:

5. Name the activities and relationships of your life for which this point is important.

6. What do you believe God's wisdom is directing you to do regarding these activities and relationships?

7. Prayerfully write your commitment to the Lord. Say specifically what you will do to implement His wisdom in your life and when you will do it.

8. Share your commitment with a fellow believer or leader, and act to fulfill it. You will be blessed not merely in knowing God's wisdom, but in doing it (see James 1:5–8, 12–25).

Appendix 1/Introduction to Old Testament Poetry

At a very early date poetry became part of the written literature of the Hebrew people. Many scholars believe the song of Moses and the song of Miriam (Ex. 15:1–21), celebrating the destruction of Pharaoh's army in the sea, is the oldest existing Hebrew hymn or poetic work, dating perhaps from the 12th century B.C. Three of the greatest poetic masterpieces of the Old Testament are the Song of Deborah (Judges 5); the Song of the Bow—David's lament over the death of Saul and Jonathan (2 Sam. 1:17–27)—and the Burden of Nineveh (Nah. 1:10—3:19).

Approximately forty percent of the Old Testament is written in poetry. This includes entire books (except for short prose sections), such as Job, Psalms, Proverbs, the Song of Solomon, and Lamentations. Large portions of Isaiah, Jeremiah, and the Minor Prophets are also poetic in form and content. Many scholars consider the Book of Job to be not only the greatest poem in the Old Testament but also one of the greatest poems in all literature.

The three main divisions of the Old Testament—the Law, the Prophets, and the Writings—contain poetry in successively greater amounts. Only seven Old Testament books—Leviticus, Ruth, Ezra, Nehemiah, Esther, Haggai, and Malachi—appear to have no poetic lines.

Thought Parallelism

Poetic elements such as assonance, alliteration, meter, and rhyme—so common to poetry as we know it today—occur rarely in Hebrew poetry; these are not essential ingredients of Old Testament poetry. Instead, the essential formal characteristic of Hebrew poetry is parallelism. This is a construction in which the content of one line is repeated, contrasted, or advanced by the content of the next—a type of sense rhythm characterized by thought arrangement rather than by word arrangement or rhyme. The three main types of parallelism in biblical poetry are synonymous, antihetic, and synthetic.

Synonymous parallelism occurs when a parallel segment repeats an idea found in the previous segment. With this technique a kind of paraphrase is involved; line two restates the same thought found in line one, by using equivalent expressions. Examples of synonymous parallelism are found in Genesis 4:23; "Adah and Zillah, hear my voice;/Wives of Lamech, listen to my speech!/For I have killed a man for wounding me/Even a young man for hurting me." Another example is found in Psalm 2:4: "He who sits in the heavens shall laugh;/The Lord shall hold them in derision." Yet a third example is Psalm 51:2–3: "Wash me thoroughly from my iniquity And cleanse me from my sin./For I acknowledge my transgressions,/And my sin is always before me." (Also see Ps. 24:1–3; 103:3, 7–10; Jer. 17:10; Zech. 9:9.)

Antithetic parallelism occurs when the thought of the first line is made clearer by the opposition expressed in the second line. Examples of antithetic parallelism may be found in Psalm 1:6: "The Lord knows the way of the righteous,/But the way of the ungodly shall perish"; in Psalm 34:10: "The young lions lack and suffer hunger;/But those who seek the Lord shall not lack any good thing"; and in Proverbs 14:20: "The poor man is hated even by his own neighbor,/But the rich has many friends."

Synthetic parallelism, also referred to as climactic or cumulative parallelism, expands the idea in line one by the idea in line two. In synthetic parallelism, therefore, there is an ascending (or descending) progression, a building up of thought, with each succeeding lilne adding to the first.

Here is one good example of this poetic technique: "He shall be like a tree/Planted by the rivers of water,/That brings forth its fruit in its season,/Whose leaf also shall not wither;/ And whatever he does shall prosper" (Ps. 1:3).

Another poetic form found in the Old Testament is the alphabetical acrostic, a form used often in the Book of Psalms (Psalms 9—10; 25; 34; 37; 111; 112; 119; 145). In the alphabetical psalms the first line begins with the first letter of the Hebrew alphabet, the next with the second, and so on, until all the letters of the alphabet have been used. Thus, Psalm 119 consists of 22 groups of eight verses each. The number of groups equals the number of letters in the Hebrew alphabet. The first letter of each verse in a group is (in the original Hebrew text) that letter of the alphabet that corresponds to its position in the group. Proverbs 31:10–31 is also composed in an alphabetical acrostic.

Many of the subtleties of Hebrew poetry, such as puns and various plays on words, are virtually untranslatable into English and may be fully appreciated only by an accomplished Hebrew scholar. Fortunately, many good commentaries are available to explain to the layperson these riches of Hebrew thought.

The Bible is full of numerous figures of speech, such as metaphors and similes. For example, the psalmist metaphorically described God by saying, "The Lord is my rock and my fortress and my deliverer; My God, my strength, in whom I will trust; My shield and the horn of my salvation, my stronghold" (Ps. 18:2).

Moses gave this remarkable simile describing God's care of Israel in the wilderness: "As an eagle stirs up its nest,/Hovers over its young,/Spreading out its wings, taking them up,/Carrying them on its wings,/So the Lord alone led him" (Deut. 32:11–12).

Such figures of speech are not to be interpreted literally but as poetic symbolism for God. He is the firm ground of life and a solid defense against evil. The worshiper sings for joy because of His protecting presence and the soaring power of His loving care.

Excerpted from "Poetry," in *Nelson's New Illustrated Bible Dictionary,* Ronald Youngblood, Gen. Ed. (Nashville: Thomas Nelson, 1995), 1012–1013.

Appendix 2/Introduction to Proverbs and to Wisdom Literature

The Book of Proverbs is one of the "wisdom books" of the Old Testament, containing instructions on many of the practical matters of daily life. The proverb was a familiar literary form in all ancient cultures; it was a very suitable device for collecting and summarizing the wisdom of the centuries. But the Book of Proverbs has one important difference: it points the believer to God with instructions on how to live a holy, upright life.

Structure of the Book. The Book of Proverbs has the longest title of any Old Testament book, covering the first six verses of chapter one. The author introduces himself as a teacher, one of the wise men of Israel, who has written this book as a manual of instruction on the ways of wisdom. His declaration, "The fear of the Lord is the beginning of knowledge" (1:7), summarizes the theme of Proverbs, a point he emphasizes again and again throughout the book.

In its 31 chapters, Proverbs discusses many practical matters to help believers live in harmony with God as well as their neighbors. Subjects covered in this wise and realistic book include how to choose the right kind of friends, the perils of adultery, the value of hard work, dealing justly with others in business, the dangers of strong drink, treating the poor with compassion, the values of strong family ties, the folly of pride and anger, and the characteristics of genuine friendship.

Scholars agree that Proverbs is a compilation of material from several different sources. This gives the book a unique internal structure. But the book itself tells us which parts are written by one author and which came from another's hand.

Authorship and Date

The name of Solomon as author is associated with the Book of Proverbs from the very beginning. Verse 1 of chapter 1 states: "The proverbs of Solomon the son of David." We also know that Solomon was noted throughout the ancient world for his superior wisdom (1 Kin. 4:29–34). Additional evidence of his authorship is found within the book itself, where Solomon is identified as author of the section from 10:1—22:16 as well as writer of chapters 25—29.

But what about those portions of Proverbs that clearly are attributed to other writers, such as "the wise" (22:17), Agur (30:1), and King Lemuel (31:1)? Although Solomon wrote a major portion of Proverbs, he did not write the entire book. Many scholars believe he wrote the basic core of Proverbs but that some writings were later added from other sources.

Another interesting fact about this book and its writing is that the second collection of proverbs attributed to Solomon (chaps. 25—29) was not added to the book until more than 200 years after his death. The heading over this material reads: "There also are proverbs of Solomon which the the men of Hezekiah king of Judah copied" (25:1). Perhaps these writings of Solomon were not discovered and inserted into the book until Hezekiah's time.

Because of the strong evidence that the Book of Proverbs is, indeed, a compilation, some scholars dismiss the idea that Solomon wrote any of the material. But evidence for his authorship of some sections is too strong to be dismissed that lightly. In its original version the book must have been written by Solomon some time during his reign from 970 B.C. to 931 B.C. Then, about 720 B.C. or later the non-Solomonic sections were added to the book.

Historical Setting

The Book of Proverbs is the classical example of the type of writing in the Old Testament known as Wisdom Literature. Other books so categorized are Job, Ecclesiastes, and the Song of Solomon. These books are called wisdom writings because they were written by a distinctive group of people in Israel's history who grappled with some of the eternal questions of life. This type of writing flourished especially during Solomon's time, and he was known as the wisest of the wise throughout the ancient world. "Thus Solomon's wisdom excelled the wisdom of all the men of the East and all the wisdom of Egypt. For he was wiser than all men . . . and his fame was in all the surrounding nations" (1 Kin. 4:30–31).

Theological Contribution

Israel's distinctive contribution to the thinking of the wise men of all nations and times is that true wisdom is centered in respect and reverence for God. This is the great underlying theme of the Book of Proverbs.

Special Considerations

In reading the Book of Proverbs, we need to make sure we do not turn these wise sayings into literal promises. Proverbs are statements of the way things generally turn out in God's world. For example, it is generally true that those who keep God's commandments will enjoy "length of days and long life" (3:2). But this should not be interpreted as an iron-clad guarantee. It is important to keep God's laws, no matter how long or short our earthly life may be.

What Is "Wisdom Literature"?

Wisdom literature is a type of literature, common to the peoples of the ancient world, that included ethical and philosophical works. The wisdom literature of the Old Testament consists of the books of Job, Proverbs, and Ecclesiastes, and certain of the psalms (Psalm 1; 19; 37; 49; 104; 107; 112; 119; 127; 128; 133; 147; 148).

In general, two principal types of wisdom are found in the wisdom literature of the Old Testament—practical and speculative. Practical wisdom consists mainly of wise sayings that offer guidelines for a successful and happy life. These are maxims of commonsense insight and observation about how intelligent people should conduct themselves.

The Book of Proverbs is a good example of practical wisdom; it encourages the pursuit of wisdom and the practice of strict discipline, hard work, and high moral standards as the way to happiness and success. Proverbs is an optimistic book. It assumes that wisdom is attainable by all who seek and follow it. The book also declares that those who keep God's moral and ethical laws will be rewarded with long life, health, possessions, respect, security, and self-control.

Speculative wisdom, such as that found in the books of Job and Ecclesiastes, goes beyond practical maxims about daily conduct. It reflects upon the deeper issues of the meaning of life, the worth and value of life, and the existence of evil in the world.

The Book of Job seeks to explain the ways of God to humankind. One of the themes of the book is the suffering of the righteous and the apparent prosperity of the wicked. The answer to such questions is that the prosperity of the wicked is brief and illusory (Job 15:21–29; 24:24) while the righteous, although presently suffering, will eventually receive God's reward.

Like the Book of Proverbs, the Book of Ecclesiastes also contains rules for living and sayings of practical wisdom. But Ecclesiastes is more than a collection of discourses and observations designed to instruct people on how to conduct their lives. Because of its skeptical and pessimistic tone, the Book of Ecclesiastes is the most "philosophical" book of the Bible. As such, it must be classified among the works of speculative wisdom.

The wisdom psalms are similar in tone and content to the books of Job and Proverbs. Some of these psalms struggle with the problem of evil and sin in the world. Others give practical advice for daily living.

Excerpted from "Proverbs, Book of" and "Wisdom Literature," in *Nelson's New Illustrated Bible Dictionary,* Ronald Youngblood, Gen. Ed. (Nashville: Thomas Nelson, 1995), 1041–1043, 1316–1317.

SPIRIT-FILLED LIFE® BIBLE DISCOVERY GUIDE SERIES

B 1 Genesis 0-8407-8515-1
B 2 Exodus, Leviticus, Numbers, Deuteronomy 0-8407-8513-5
B 3* Joshua & Judges
B 4 Ruth & Esther 0-7852-1133-0
B 5* 1 & 2 Samuel, 1 Chronicles
B 6* 1 & 2 Kings, 2 Chronicles
B 7* Ezra & Nehemiah
B 8* Job, Ecclesiastes, Song of Songs
B 9 Psalms 0-8407-8347-7
B10 Proverbs 0-7852-1167-5
B11 Isaiah 0-7852-1168-3
B12* Jeremiah, Lamentations, Ezekiel
B13 Daniel & Revelation 0-8407-2081-5
B14 Hosea, Joel, Amos, Obadiah, Jonah, Micah, Nahum, Habakkuk, Zephaniah, Haggai, Zechariah, Malachi 0-8407-2093-9
B15 Matthew, Mark, Luke 0-8407-2090-4
B16 John 0-8407-8349-3
B17 Acts 0-8407-8345-0
B18 Romans 0-8407-8350-7
B19 1 Corinthians 0-8407-8514-3
B20* 2 Corinthians, 1 & 2 Timothy, Titus 0-7852-1204-3
B21 Galatians, 1 & 2 Thessalonians 0-7852-1134-9
B22 Ephesians, Philippians, Colossians, Philemon 0-8407-8512-7
B23 Hebrews 0-8407-2082-3
B24* James, 1 & 2 Peter, 1–3 John, Jude 0-7852-1205-1
B25* Getting to the Heart of the Bible (Key Themes: Basics of Bible Study)

*In preparation.

SPIRIT-FILLED LIFE® KINGDOM DYNAMICS STUDY GUIDE SERIES

K 1 People of the Spirit: Gifts, Fruit, and Fullness of the Holy Spirit 0-8407-8431-7
K 2 Kingdom Warfare: Prayer, Spiritual Warfare, and the Ministry of Angels 0-8407-8433-3
K 3 God's Way to Wholeness: Divine Healing by the Power of the Holy Spirit 0-8407-8430-9
K 4 Life in the Kingdom: Foundations of the Faith 0-8407-8432-5
K 5 Focusing on the Future: Key Prophecies and Practical Living 0-8407-8517-8
K 6 Toward More Glorious Praise: Power Principles for Faith-Filled People 0-8407-8518-6
K 7 Bible Ministries for Women: God's Daughters and God's Work 0-8407-8519-4
K 8 People of the Covenant: God's New Covenant for Today 0-8407-8520-8
K 9 Answering the Call to Evangelism: Spreading the Good News to Everyone 0-8407-2096-3
K10 Spirit-Filled Family: Holy Wisdom to Build Happy Homes 0-8407-2085-8
K11 Appointed to Leadership: God's Principles for Spiritual Leaders 0-8407-2083-1
K12 Power Faith: Balancing Faith in Words and Work 0-8407-2094-7
K13 Race & Reconciliation: Healing the Wounds, Winning the Harvest 0-7852-1131-4
K14 Praying in the Spirit: Heavenly Resources for Praise and Intercession 0-7852-1141-1

OTHER SPIRIT-FILLED LIFE® STUDY RESOURCES

Spirit-Filled Life® Bible, available in several bindings and in NKJV and KJV.

Spirit-Filled Life® Bible for Students

Hayford's Bible Handbook 0-8407-8359-0